Black American Money 2

Dr. Boyce Watkins

Copyright © 2017 Dr. Boyce Watkins

All rights reserved.

ISBN: 1544111711
ISBN-13: 9781544111711

DEDICATION

This book is dedicated to my grandmother Felicia who taught me the value of being a good financial steward.

CONTENTS

1	Why Black People Need to Save Money	5
2	The Stock Market is for Black Folks Too	15
3	How to Avoid Going for Broke: The Vin Baker Story	39
4	Fight the Power: Are We Going About it the Wrong Way?	47
5	Yes, Our Children are Watching	52
6	The Importance of Economic Partnerships	71
7	Are We Really a Broke People?	85
8	Mainstream America and the Black Dollar	101
9	Let's Talk About Money in Real Terms: An Interview with the Breakfast Club	119
10	Creating Generational Wealth	174

Foreword

A few years ago, I wrote *Black American Money*. The book was my humble attempt to help black people better understand the nuances, power, and relevancy of our money. Too often, our dollars leave our purses, our pockets, and our communities. This has left many of us feeling as if we cannot control our economic destinies. This, then, begs the question of: Who controls the future of black America? Is it the politicians? Is it Wall Street? Some may take a slightly different approach and ask: Is our destiny defined by religion, luck, or something else?

It is my firm belief that the future of black America is controlled by none other than black people themselves. Look in the mirror. Yes, I am talking about you.

The truth about America is that it is built on a set of rules and procedures that give advantages to some and setbacks to others. Opportunities exist, but only for those who are skilled, well-read, ambitious, creative, and unified. *Black American Money 2* will provide you with numerous opportunities to learn about your personal finances, the stock market, and preparing our next generations to be successful.

Many years ago, when I was being kicked out of my apartment for not being able to pay the rent, I drove across the country hoping to get into The Ohio State University. Driving in the middle of the night, I had everything I owned in the van with me, including my basketball, which lay on the dashboard. At that time, all I had was hope, for I'd effectively lost everything: My income, my relationship, my scholarship, and my place to live.

It is often during our darkest moments that we learn to generate our own electricity. During that difficult and lonely experience, I found that I could be stronger than I'd ever expected, and that the only way for me to improve my condition was through hard work, focus, education, and never giving up. It was during that time that the Boyce Watkins you know came to life. Like a diamond in a mine, it took unbelievable amounts of pressure for my spirit to learn how to shine.

I've never been good at lying, so I simply try not to do it. I write from the heart, and by learning how to love myself over time, I've become comfortable with speaking truth, even if it creates discomfort in those around me.

I have the same fears as everyone else, but over time, I've learned that living with fear is part of being black in America. My claim to so-called fearlessness is not built on the idea that I am devoid of the same concerns as everyone else, it's just that I've learned to feel the fear and move forward anyway. The demon of fear might be inside my vehicle, but I keep it in the trunk, not in the driver's seat.

For us to build the nation and community we desire, we must all find our own version of fearlessness. We must stop believing that receiving love from condescending white liberals is the only thing protecting us from slavery. We must stop believing that working for our oppressors will give us our only pathway to survival. We must stop playing checkers and learn that the world is run by those who master the game of chess.

Black people are the strongest and most capable people on this planet, but unfortunately, our greatness is often pushed into the shadows of unimaginable terror, trauma, and apprehension that leaves us spiritually paralyzed. It's hard to climb mountains when you have no legs, and many of us receive amputations at birth.

This book is an exploration of the ideas that will challenge us and make us stronger as we enter a new chapter in America. This collection of essays reflect my own raw truth, unfiltered, and void of any corporate entity. The fact is that it is only by coming together and confronting the chains that bind us that black people can be strong and united in this generation and the next.

We must plot, plan, prepare, teach, build, and grow our way to the mountain top for there is no elevator that will get us where we need to be.

That's what this book is all about.

Dr. Boyce Watkins

Dr. Boyce Watkins

CHAPTER 1

WHY BLACK PEOPLE NEED TO SAVE MONEY

Chattel slavery ended over a century ago, yet many of us are still enslaved. We are enslaved to our finances because, at some point in our lives, we were not taught about the value of money, credit, and saving. This has led to too many of our people who are beholden to a system that they are unfamiliar with—a system that has created generations that are accustomed to living pay check to pay check.

Too many Americans are one pay check or one job loss away from being wiped out financially. Specifically, when it comes to unemployment numbers issued by the Bureau of Labor Statistics, there was a tale of two ethnicities. White Americans saw their unemployment rate decline in every demographic (women, men and teens), while African Americans saw their rate rise in every single category.

The overall national unemployment rate dropped from 9% to 8.6%. But the differentials conceal a sharp and problematic racial undertone as it pertains to black unemployment. White men saw their unemployment rate decline the most, dropping from 7.9% to 7.3%, while black men endured a spike from 16.2% to an especially disturbing 16.5%.

White women were the beneficiaries of racial inequality as well. The white female unemployment rate dropped from 7% to 6.9% (the lowest rate of any racial/gender group), while black female unemployment rose from 12.6% to 12.9%.

The racial gap was also present among teenagers. White teen unemployment dropped from 21.8% to 21.3%, while black teen unemployment rose from 37.8% to 39.6%.

Across the board, white unemployment dropped from 8% to 7.6%, while black unemployment rose from 15.1% to 15.5%.

One of the reasons why it is important to support black business is because of numbers like the ones I've mentioned in this article. Malcolm X reminded us long ago that if African Americans do not own their own businesses, we will always be subject to glaring disparities in unemployment rates, mainly because the jobs are being controlled and granted by the descendants of our historical oppressors.

New paradigms are in order to help us to obtain empowerment in a capitalist society. If we continue to attack the old issues in the same old ways, we will continue to get the same depressing results. What's even more insulting is that after this recession is over, black unemployment will likely remain just as high as white unemployment is right now. In other words, we will be expected to celebrate the circumstances that white Americans now consider to be entirely unbearable. It's time for a change.

There are ways that you can improve your current financial situation. It does not require extensive study or research; however, it does require a willingness to learn and to exercise restraint. In fact, there are several things that might be helpful to you in your effort to save money, to build wealth, and to get out of whatever rutty financial situation you might feel like you're stuck in right now.

One of the things they say about saving money, which is an old saying, but I love it, is that you should save your money so your money can save you. If you don't save, if you're buried in debt, if you have incredibly high expenses, and you have one source of income, then what you are effectively making yourself into is a financial slave. If you're not careful you will end up in a life that you don't want or in a life that's controlled by somebody else, doing things that you do not want to do, and in situations that you don't want to be in.

You have to understand that you played some part in putting yourself in every situation that you're in. There are a billion different situations you could be in right now other than the ones that you're in. Always remember that those decisions, in terms of putting ourselves where we want to be, are ultimately made by us. That's a scary thought, but, at the same time, it's an empowering thought. It means that you shape your destiny; you shape your outcomes.

What I want to do is give you some tips that might help you break out of that rut. I taught finance for about 20 years at different universities and one of the things I learned about money over those years is that saving money and money management are 90% about personality. It's mostly psychological. It's not just about what you know or knowing how to do it. It's about doing what you know you're supposed to do.

I call it the fat gym teacher's paradox where you got these people that teach gym and can tell you everything you need to know about being healthy, but they're weighing 400 pounds and eating cheeseburgers every day. It's not because they don't know what to do; it's because they just don't want to do it.

Here are some simple tips that can get you on the pathway to saving your money, so that you don't end up in a situation that makes you feel like you are financially strapped or that you're an economic slave.

Number One: Use Auto Deduct

When it comes to saving money, you want auto deduct. Have your money automatically taken out of your personal checking account, so that you don't see the money before it goes into your savings. What happens is that some of us have formed the bad habit of being spendaholics. I'm a recovering spendaholic.

I have no problem admitting that. If you are not intentional or not careful then you can get in the habit of feeling that whatever money is in your pocket can burn a hole in your pocket. You ever heard anybody say that? Well, maybe it's okay to let the money burn a hole in your pocket. To prevent that from happening, you just need to keep your pockets light. In other words, if it is not available to you immediately then it is more difficult for you to spend.

If you have some money taken out in advance and put into a special account then you will have a hard time getting access to it. You might even forget about it; that's a great way to save money.

Also, having a little jar in your house where you throw your spare change in when you come through the door is another good way to save a little bit of money. It's not going to be enough to buy you a house, but it might be enough to pay for some groceries in case you need some extra spending money.

Number Two: Pay Yourself First

When it comes to saving money, you want to pay yourself first. Don't get in the habit of saving whatever is leftover because what happens is that if you're on a tight budget, you won't have anything left over. You should prioritize the things that matter to you and there's nothing that should matter to you more than *you*. That means that you put the savings at the top of the budget, not at the bottom. Take that savings out first and then pay the bills with whatever is left. This will prevent overspending.

Number Three: Stop Giving Away Your Money

The best way to keep your money is to not give it away. Don't give your money away to these companies that are getting you hooked on impulsive spending and trying to trick you into buying things that you know you don't need anyway, stuff that's severely overpriced. They pay $12 to make some headphones over in Malaysia and then sell them to you for 250 bucks. Think about that stuff.

Dr. Tommy Whittler, an expert marketing professor at DePaul University, constantly reminds us that impulsive spending prevents us from saving and acquiring wealth. He basically says that companies spend marketing money for the explicit purposes of playing with your mind; it is the most effective way to get you to let go of your money, even when you don't even know what happened or why.

In other words, someone has studied our spending habits and they've got you figured out before you even walk through the door. So, you want to make sure that you're smarter than the systems that are designed to manipulate you, oppress you, and ultimately leave you broke.

Number Four: Avoid High-Interest Credit Cards

Credit cards are a huge saving's killer. Believe it or not, many credit card companies charge you just insane amounts of interest. Start eliminating your high-interest credit cards. If you have three types of debt: one is lower interest, one is medium, and one is high, try to get everything into the low interest category. That means maybe borrowing from the low interest group to pay off the high interest group. There is nothing wrong with that. Or you can use a little bit of your savings to get rid of that credit card debt.

Credit card debt usually isn't good for you because a lot of credit card debt is because we spend on things that we don't even really need. Credit card companies, remember, are not in business to help you out. They're in business to make money off of you.

Number Five: Identify Sources of Extra Income

At one point in my life, I realized that I needed extra income. I found it was easier to save money when I had more money. See, if you make more money then you don't have to necessarily save as much because you have more disposable income. You could just use the extra money as your savings, especially if find and secure additional streams of revenue.

There's nothing better in life than to have a side hustle. Let's say you make $3000 a month and you get an opportunity to make an extra $500 a month. That $500 a month can make a big difference and can lead to greater financial comfort and security. I mean, if you save $500 a month that's $6000 a year. That's going to add up over time.

One of the things I did in order to save more money was I actually said, "Okay, you know what? I'm just going to find a way to make more money on the side." I figured it out. I had a side hustle. The side hustle was paying for all the extra stuff and it was also going into my savings; I didn't even have to really touch my original budget. That's the secret that you don't hear from a lot of these financial experts because they always assume that saving money means you have to chop down your expenses. Well, yes, that's one way to save money, but another way to save money is just make more money and then just make sure the extra money goes into your savings.

Once you begin to implement these practices, you will begin to see your finances improve. It is not as difficult as some may make it appear and the reality is that it is critical to our success and survival as a people.

This reminds me of an article in *Mother Jones* that pretty much explained that the 100 richest white people in the world or in America have more wealth than the entire African American community put together. That's atrocious. That's a legacy of slavery, legacy of Jim Crow, legacy of oppression, a legacy of rampant discrimination, criminalization, and terrorism.

No question about it. White people, if you're reading, you need to understand that this is why black folks have a hard time getting down with you. You won't acknowledge or concede what your ancestors did and how you benefited from it. I'm not going to forgive or forget until my ancestors are vindicated in terms of having the wealth returned that belongs to us.

Now, with that being said, I saw an article by Antonio Moore. He and others have claimed that black wealth just doesn't exist. Some people assert that even if you throw in celebrities, athletes, and everybody else, black people just have nothing. We're just done; we're dead broke (I will talk about this in greater detail in a later chapter); and we don't have nothing.

I'm a little bit concerned about that assessment for a couple of reasons. Number one, I hate the idea. I hate us falling for this notion that the only way we, as black people, can ever have anything, ever get ahead, ever accumulate any resources in this world, is if white people decide to come together and hook us up, right? I just can't buy into that false narrative. That's a significant problem in my mind because I don't think they're ever going to *save us*. The cavalry is not coming, you're going to have to build for yourself.

Second of all, I think we have to be very cautious about taking a snapshot and thinking that everything is in the snapshot. You can't judge the next 300 years based on what you see right now. I will tell you this, if every black parent, for example, made sure that their child learned entrepreneurship and if every black parent made sure that their child learned technology and if every black parent made sure that their child got a superior education, which is usually going to come from home—it's not going to come from a school system—then black wealth would literally flip everything on its head within a generation or two because people that tend to have the most education and the most information also tend to have the most resources.

Let me place this into its proper context.

Even though black people, generationally, don't have as much as white people, we still have something to work with. Part of the reason that we think we don't have anything is because white people have so much. White Americans have more wealth than almost anybody on earth. Why is that relevant?

Just recently, China and the European Union passed the United States in terms of total gross domestic product, which is the productivity of all the goods and services that a country produces. In other words, we are third on the list now behind China and the European Union which really isn't one country because it's a group of countries that came together to form a union.

So here's the problem. When we compare ourselves to white people, we have to think more globally. For example, when you say something like, "Black American wealth does not exist," or "There is no black wealth in America," you have to think in terms of why that assessment is being made. That's like saying Jamaica doesn't exist which is illogical. In fact, we have more wealth in the Black community than the GDP of Jamaica.

It might be helpful if I share countries whose GDPs are less than that of Black America. We could literally buy the Gross Domestic Product of all these countries. Let me go down the list and as I do, it just might surprise you and make you rethink many of our widely held and often repeated beliefs about black money: Iran, Australia, Thailand, Taiwan, Egypt, Nigeria, Poland, Pakistan, Argentina, the Philippines, the Netherlands, Malaysia, South Africa, Colombia, United Arab Emirates, Algeria,

Bangladesh, Viet Nam, Iraq, Venezuela, Belgium, Switzerland, Sweden, Singapore, Kazakhstan, Chile, Hong Kong, Romania, Austria, Peru, Norway, Ukraine, Czech Republic, Qatar, Portugal, Kuwait, Greece, Myanmar, Morocco, Israel, Denmark, Ireland, Finland, Sri Lanka, and I could keep going.

I could literally keep adding countries to help illustrate this fact. Yet, don't get me wrong, this is not to say that we should pretend like everything is all wonderful and ideal in the black community.

That isn't what I'm trying to say, and I am also not saying that my esteemed friends are crazy or wrong. There's a lot to be mad about if you're black, and it is unwise to suggest that government involvement should not and can't be part of the solution.

From my vantage point, I don't see the government being part of the solution, at least not right now—maybe in 50 years or maybe in 30 years, white people will wake up and say, "We *do* owe these people reparations because what we did to them was some pretty horrible stuff."

But, we can't sit here and pretend like we don't have anything to work with.

As I always tell people in the Black Wealth Bootcamp, no white man has ever told you that you can't pick up your cell phone and do some research and learn things on your cell phone. No white man has ever told you that you can't learn how to start a small business. Just because he won't give you a loan doesn't mean that you can't start a business. That's what they call bootstrapping your business.

There is no law, written or unwritten, stating that you can't buy stocks on the same stock market that others buy stocks on. I can show you mathematically how to do so. I have been a finance professor for 23 years. I taught my first finance class when I was 22, so I know money pretty well, and I leverage that knowledge to position our people to be successful.

For example, let's say I started investing at the young age of 22—which I did not do—and I bought $100 worth of stock every month in the stock market. Any stocks that I pick, no matter what I pick, would generate over $100,000, $200,000 to $300,000 in wealth from just from $100 a month. And if you do that over the course of let's say 30 years or over the course of your lifetime then your child won't have to start off at the beginning at ground zero.

Your child can start off with capital, with a capital base, and if they now how to intelligently apply that capital then they can build the wealth they need to thrive.

So my point here—again, I'm not trying to be disparaging because Antonio is my friend and Yvette Carnell is my friend; he is a brilliant lawyer and Yvette is a social commentator, a brilliant commentator—is that we must empower ourselves.

I'm a finance professor. I know how money works; I know where money comes from; I know how all of that happens, and I can tell you that we are dipping into a doom and gloom mindset when we believe that the only way we can ever get caught up on any level is waiting for white folks.

I ain't waiting for white folks. I just ain't.

And you know what? I tell you what, I see a whole lot of people I know who embrace entrepreneurship in their families; they made something out of nothing. They might not have as much money as wealthy white people, but they got more money than most white people. Most white people look at their business and say, "Wow, I wish I had what you had." I know how much most white people make. Let's say the average white person makes $50,000 - $60,000 a year. I know a whole lot of black folks who started off with nothing, but who found a way to make several hundred thousand dollars a year. Now that is not the same as the masses though. What we need to do as a community is start teaching our children that getting yourself successful economically is not enough.

You flip it back; you get together with other people; you form a small capital base; and you structure a business so you can begin to hire other people because wealth means nothing if you're not creating wealth for other people around you and the people who are in your community. So just keep that in mind.

Let's not get caught up in the gloom and doom of it all. Let's look at the facts. Look at the truth. Let's be honest with ourselves. At the same time, never think that 2017 is the same as 2117 or 2217 or 2317. In fact, a lot of the black wealth issue, or the black wealth challenge, could be resolved if everyone just made sure that they didn't die without life insurance. Right?

Again, you may not catch up with white folks; they got more money than almost anybody on earth, that's why it seems like you're broke. You're like the poorest kid in the richest neighborhood, but understand, compared to the global community, you're doing pretty well. At the very least, you can at least get away from destitution. There's no law saying you must be stuck in poverty. Nothing. I don't care what anybody says. There's nothing saying you have to be in poverty. NOTHING.

I seriously believe that if you study what is in this book and put it into practice, then you will have the foundation for receiving the core information that you would receive at a finance program at any major university, including Harvard or Yale.

CHAPTER 2

THE STOCK MARKET IS FOR BLACK FOLKS TOO

There is this strange idea that somehow the stock market is only for white people or people who work for corporations who invest on their behalf. Starting right now, we need to stop giving credence to these ideas. They hurt us and our ability to produce generational wealth.

There's a lot of interest in the stock market and for good reason. There's a lot of wealth that's built from investing. The people who tend to make the most money the easiest way are people who are taught investing at an early age. I can tell you that your recently inaugurated 45th President of the United States, Donald Trump, is teaching his children, little Barron, little Ivanka and little JJ, (whatever his other kids' names are) how to invest.

He's teaching them how to make money just like your parents taught you how to make money and like you're teaching your kids how to make money, but he's teaching them in a way that is going to put them in the driver's seat and not that of the passenger.

My Ph.D. in finance gives me the ability to understand at a

microscopic, DNA level, how financial markets work, how wealth building works, how wealth accumulation works, and how all of that works to enhance the lives of others. My goal, or my job, is to talk to you about it so that you are informed and you can't say, "Well, I would have done things differently if somebody had taught me differently."

You're here; you're reading this book now and I'm going to teach you everything that your parents might not have taught you and give you a taste of how things can change in your life moving forward.

Before I delve further into discussing the stock market, let me briefly explain why I am so passionate about black wealth.

I started the Black Business School to create a low-cost, high-quality, alternative to an overpriced college education. A college education can leave people in debt; we don't leave anyone in debt at the Black Business School. Our students walk away with a surplus of information because we teach people how to build. We are big on building for the next generation.

Our physical location is at Simmons College of Kentucky. It is an HBCU where we've recently launched The Dr. Boyce Watkins Economic Empowerment Institute. As we build for the future, it will be our physical location if you ever want to take a class there. I am sharing this information with you in *Black American Money 2* because it reflects what can happen when we become a forward-thinking people as it relates to our economic resources.

We have to utilize various platforms—physical and digital—that will best reach Black people. The 21st century landscape calls for 21st century learning and we need to be prepared.

Think of this as being analogous to taking medication that may have worked 30 years ago, but, because of research and development, there are now more effective options.

You have the old school medication where it might make you better, but it might also kill you at the same time. Over time, we will continue to get better medications and we will eventually get to the place where nano-medicine can precisely pinpoint where the problem is and fix it.

So for black people, our medication, our economic medication, cannot be broad-based; the tide will lift all boats. It can't be trickle-down economics; it must be precise. It must be based specifically on what we've gone through, where we are, where we are currently trying to go and what we need to get there. In fact, even to use the medical analogy, there are medications that work differently with black people than with white people.

Well, the same thing is true with economic medication. I hate saying this; and maybe I'm the first person to tell you this; and I don't know if I sound radical by saying this, but you aren't white.

You aren't white.

Let me say that again: You're not white. Now, why do I need to tell you that you are not white?

You're like, "Wait a minute, Boyce, you're way off. You already know I'm not white." Well, the reason I have to tell you you're not white is because you still believe in this illusion of American inclusiveness. This is not because America can't be inclusive, not because America can't be diverse, and not because America can't get better, but because there is no real evidence to say that America even has a desire to be fully inclusive.

We are often taught to go to the predominantly white school (which is fine because I went to The Ohio State University where I earned my Ph.D.). What we are not taught is how to maintain our sense of self-worth when others are trying to erode it.

For example, you go to class with other people who don't look like you, and you all graduate and you've got better grades than them and you all go apply for the same job. Yet, you don't get the job. Or if you get the job, you don't get the same pay. Or if you get the pay, you don't get the same promotional opportunities. Or if you get the promotional opportunities, you find that the sacrifice that you have to make spiritually is so deep, insidious, and painful that you wake up every morning stressed.

You get to about 35 years old and you wonder, "What the hell did I just waste my time doing? Whose dream am I following? Whose plan or whose vision was this? This wasn't mine. If I could have built my own vision then it definitely wouldn't have been this."

That's what I went through. I achieved the so-called "black American dream." I achieved the integration dream, the affirmative action dream, and the assimilation dream. I was in school all throughout my 20s. In fact, I didn't get my first job until

I was 31 years old, but that first job made up for all of the jobs I didn't get.

I was making about $120,000 a year, or something very close to that, and that was pretty cool. I could be proud of what I was and what I'd accomplished, but I wasn't happy.

I wasn't doing work that had any real meaning or real value; I wasn't helping my own people. I was dealing with a bunch of pricks. I worked with people who I didn't like, and I said, "I got to get the hell up out of here. This isn't right, my spirit is not right."

I've always been a little bit of a loner; it's good to be a little bit of a loner because you come to your own perception of the world that's not tainted by what other people have been led to believe. I'd sit up in my home, in a neighborhood where there weren't any black people, and I would think, "Man, this doesn't seem right. I'm successful, but I don't feel successful. I've made it, but I don't feel like I've made it. I'm supposed to be powerful, but I feel powerless."

That's what led me down the journey of thinking about the connection between wealth and power, how to get real power, and what that looks like.

I share this with you because I want you to understand that when it comes to the stock market, you are not powerless. It is not some mystical thing that was designed for other people and not for you.

It all can begin with just $5.00. Yes, you read that correctly. For the amount that you might pay for a value meal, a large coffee or a pair of socks, you can begin your journey to economic freedom.

To get you started on your investing journey, I want to explain what I call my $5 a day investment plan. Since I came up with it, I named it after me. It's called the *Dr. Boyce Watkins $5 a day Wealth Building Plan.*

It starts with understanding compound interest.

It's fun to use the magic of compound interest to really show people amazing things in terms of what you can actually accomplish with your own money. Have you ever heard a story about how somebody walked from New York to LA.

You, like me, probably thought, "How in the world, do you walk from New York to LA; is that even impossible?" People have done it; people have traveled that distance. All of them, initially, started by putting one foot in front of the other. Even if they were walking slowly, mathematically, all they had to do was just keep walking—one step at a time. Eventually, they would all get to their destination, right? Are you following my logic here?

Well, wealth building is similar to this. It's only mysterious in the sense that you're like, "Wait a minute. A person can only do so much every day and yet, actually, accumulate enough to get into the 1% by the time that they're done?" Yes!

Well, let me show you.

Let's go through the math. First, it is worth noting that the SMP 500, which is a measuring stick of 500 of the largest companies in America on the stock market, went up 181% during the time that President Obama was in office.

So if you were a stock market investor, you're very happy with the Obama presidency because the stock market did really well. The Dow Jones Industrial Average went up 148% and the NASDAQ went up 284.5%. That's almost triple from where it started.

Have you ever heard somebody say something like, "We bought this house for 90,000 and now, 20 years later, it's worth 210,000." And they're proud of that; they think that's really cool, right? 90 to 210 is not even triple. That's about two and a half times the original value. It sounds impressive, right? Think again.

Over an eight year period, the average NASDAQ investor saw their money almost triple. That means if someone invested 10,000 in the market that 10,000 turned into about 28,400, right? Yes.

Regardless of who is in the White House, this is going to continue to rise based on all of the indicators that I see. Why?

Well, because presidents prioritize stock market performance in their agenda. If the stock market crashes, they get together that morning and have a meeting with economic advisors to say, "What can we do to make the stock market improve?"

Now, imagine if they did that with black American problems? Imagine if we lived in a world—this is me fantasizing here—where they would say, "My God, this year 750 people were murdered on the south side of Chicago. That's a national crisis. Let us meet this morning to solve this problem."

Can you imagine if they had meetings like that? How quickly would they be able to clean up the violence in Chicago? But they don't clean it up because they don't care. I digress.

Here is how this connects back to the stock market. Well, when it comes to the stock market crash, when investors are losing money, they give the loss in the stock market A1, top tier priority. So this is going to continue under Trump most likely. If it does drop, believe me, they're going to do everything they can to keep it from happening. That is a benefit to you if you're an investor.

Politicians may or may not help the working class, but they always take care of their own people. They take care of people who own property; they take care of people who own businesses; they take care of people who own stock. The tax code is even structured to benefit those who do those things. They incentivize activity in the economy with taxation.

If they want you to do something over here, they'll say, "Okay, we're going to give you a lower tax if you do this." For example, in investing, you pay a lower tax if you invest long term than if you invest short term. That's because they don't want people to be short term investors.

Why? Well, because short term investing and day trading make the markets go up and down and create what they call volatility. So they don't want volatility; they want smooth, well-functioning markets that go up over time. So they incentivize you to be a long term investor.

What else? They also want you to own a house. They wanted you to believe that owning a home was the American dream, so what did they do? They said, "Well, we're going to let you write off the interest that you pay on your mortgage. We're going to give you special tax treatment on the mortgage."

They want corporations and business owners to do well, so Reaganomics led to their saying, "Okay, we're going to create preferential tax treatment for people who own businesses." So they create the tax code to benefit certain people and get them to do certain things. The tax code is designed to benefit those who own instead of rent.

If you're a renter, you don't get tax breaks for renting, but if you're an owner, there's a whole lot of tax breaks. You get benefits for running companies instead of working for other people. You get tax benefits from producing rather than consuming products. You get tax benefits for lending as opposed to borrowing. You get tax benefits for investing rather than spending.

Let's go down that list. You've got owners: people who own land, who own companies, who produce products, who make loans, and who invest. Then you've got the people who rent.

Now, I want you to think about which side of this fence you were raised on. Think about people who rent apartments instead of trying to own homes or people who work for other people instead of starting a business. Do you know people who consume? Lastly, think about those who borrow, or who go deep in debt, as opposed to those who actually loan money to people who are going in debt—spenders rather than investors.

Which category do you think that most of us are in? Most of us were raised to spend and/or to consume, right?

Often, where you end up economically is most likely determined by where you started. Now, let's go deeper into this. Imagine a graph that shows the stock market performance over the eight year time period that President Obama was running for office up until the time that he left. The stock market kept going up.

In 2014, Obama said that buying stocks was a good deal for the American people. Imagine that he had a press conference and people were saying, "Whoa, wait a minute, the stock market lost money, Mr. President. All of the big money billionaires are blowing up your phone because they want to yell at you because the stock market's not performing and we know you work for them, so we need you to do something."

So, hypothetically, he says, "Well, you know buying stocks is a potentially good deal because the stock market has declined." Upon hearing this, people start buying; the demand starts going up, and prices start going up and up and up and up and up. This scenario illustrates the mechanisms that drive market performance.

Yet, there's a problem that we have in our community. A lot of people have a fear of the stock market. Deeply afraid of the market, they think that you have to be rich to buy stock, which isn't true. This is a $5 a day plan. If you can't afford $5 a day, start with the $1 a day plan or the $2 a day plan and work your way up, or maybe you can get some of your friends to pool your money together and do something.

Next, what else? People in our community tend to think, quite erroneously, that you also have to have a lot of formal education to buy stocks. That's because people who run the markets, or those who do all of this stuff, are trying to impress you because they're trying to get you to think that they're smarter than you, so they often use a lot of fancy, long words.

One time, I heard an investment advisor on TV explaining how to build wealth to somebody. He was a very polished, poised brother.

Now, mind you again, I'm a finance professor with years of expertise, so I know this stuff pretty well, and I was listening to him talk and I said, "My God, that poor lady, she's sitting there staring at him pretending like she understands what he's saying, but I know she doesn't understand what he's saying because I can't halfway keep up with what he's saying."

I could tell what he was doing; he was using a bunch of words that he didn't fully understand because he wanted to impress her to make her think that he was smart.

It reminded me of Damon. Anybody remember Damon Wayans on *Living Color*? He played the guy who was in prison who memorized the dictionary so that he could use long words?

"The antecedent of the pronoun is a subordination of the predicate." Remember that? The brother on TV was like that, and a lot of investment advisors do that. They really will throw out crazy words to confuse you, and it's also a way that they make you feel insignificant or inferior.

It's a method that can be used to extract money from you because they make you think that they can see things that they can't really see. It just adds to the confusion.

Besides the fact that people may find the market confusing, some also think the market is corrupt. Well, there is a little bit of corruption in the stock market, but the US markets are actually among the least corrupt in the world, and they actually have the Securities and Exchange Commission (SEC), which was put in place so that white people can't rob other white people.

If they can't rob each other then they're not really going to be able to easily rob you. Trust me, I know you want to believe that horrible things are going to happen every time black people try to do something, and I understand. I mean we had Black Wall Street; we had all of these other atrocities that have occurred, but I'm telling you that the coast is clear. You can come out now; you don't have to be scared.

Don't get me wrong, there's still stuff out there; there's stuff going on, I mean we've got Trump in the White House.

However, there are lots of people, black people like you and me, regular working class people, who have become multimillionaires and the beautiful thing is that they often move in silence.

Let that marinate.

These millionaires move in silence. You don't even know that they have all this money because they're not being flashy; they're not trying to wear their money; they're not trying to drive their money; and they're not trying to impress people that don't matter. Instead, they're driving little regular cars, wearing regular clothes, living in regular houses, and living regular lives. It is fair to say that they do very basic stuff.

They don't go deep in debt when they go to college; they don't spend money to impress people. They start businesses; they save consistently, and they invest. Next thing you know, they're passing over a million bucks down to their kids.

Now, you are probably thinking that this sounds great, but aren't there risks involved? A lot of people think that the market's a great place to lose money. Why? Well, because you see all of the ups and downs on the day to day market. For some, that might be a deterrent.

Warren Buffet, one of the greatest investors of all time explained it very clearly. He said, "If you're not prepared to own a stock for at least 10 years, then you shouldn't even think about owning it for 10 minutes. If you own stock long term, a lot of those ups and downs don't matter anymore."

Here are some key facts to think about. Trillions of dollars in wealth are being created on the stock market; the rich are getting richer. The reason the rich are getting richer is mainly because they own stocks and own businesses.

Middle class people will buy homes. This is the bulk of their wealth. If you're middle class, a significant percentage of your wealth is in your home or maybe it is in your retirement. If you want to be upper class, you have to step your game up a notch. Instead of owning one home, wealthy people find a way to buy two and three homes.

Also, instead of just owning a house, they also put money into the stock market or they own businesses. Instead of working for people, they own companies. Instead of being an employee, they are employers.

So that's how the rich get richer. That's what the 1% does. Middle class people own homes and poor people own nothing unfortunately. But there are ways to be an owner no matter who you are, no matter what your income level is. So what are some keys?

Well, number one there's a formula. There's a way that wealth builders build wealth. Most regular people are never taught this, and I'm going to explain why.

Too often, we want to believe that we're powerless because we really want to believe that we have no choice; we want to believe that we're incapable of accomplishing anything. We love to find a hole in any solution that comes along. I call them negro naysayers, you know, people that find a problem for every solution.

It's almost like they're playing defense against hope and prosperity and possibility, right? Like you say, "Well, you know, if we go that way, we can..." They will immediately respond,"Nuh-uh, nope, that ain't going to work." You may then try a different approach. "Let's try this. . . " They chime in, "No, that's ain't going to work."

We all know people like that and investing in the stock market may lead to some push back. Every time you start a business, they're just going to burn it down, so you don't start one.

I don't like that because what that's really saying to me, unfortunately, is that some of us have been trained to think a specific way. We don't really want to learn how it's possible to do some of this for ourselves because we use despair, doubt, and hopelessness as excuses for laziness.

When you don't believe something's doable, then you don't even try. That gives you an excuse to not even try. How many people do you know like that? There are people who are so hopeless that they don't even try.

And if you say, "Well, you know, I know you're broke, I know you're struggling and everything, but you know you had $200 and you could have saved that and you could have done this or that instead." Or if you say, "You know, you could have gotten a job at the such and such," they have an excuse as to why not.

They fight you every step of the way. They're like, "Well, no, I was sick that day. My foot was hurting. It was sore and didn't want to go out there. It was too cold outside; I'm not going to work." They'll find an excuse.

This is the negro naysayer mentality. It is like a psychological addiction to what I would call strugglenomics. Strugglenomics, to me, is when you are blindly committed to the struggle, and don't question it at all, not even with the language that you use. People will often say, "Well, it's a struggle out here. It's hard out here."

I don't really want to think about my life as a struggle. I'd rather win. But, if we have to use the battle symbol for life then let's be victors. I'm going to win because I come from the greatest group of people in the history of this world.

We are the mothers and fathers of the Earth, as (the late) Dr. Frances Cress Welsing said, "We are the parents of the universe, so you can't stop me. You can't stop me." That's when I tap into the God spirit. I don't mean to get all crazy with y'all, but I'm dead serious. In my mind, I think, "Well, no, no no, this struggle, so-called struggle, is an opportunity for us to say, 'We overcame.'"

You know how they say, "We shall overcome," well we ain't even overcome yet. We have not overcome hardly anything, but when we do overcome then we can start singing and say, "Look at what we built and we did it with nothing."

That to me is black power; that's black pride. Why does this matter and how does it connect to investing in the stock market?

If you want to obtain something, you must first believe that it is possible. As such, I pay more attention to self-made millionaires, not the people that were given everything. I'm talking about people who started with very little and accumulated a lot over time.

This leads to the biggest question that many of us must ask ourselves. At some point, you have to be willing to do some soul searching and answer this critical question:

How am I going to make some money?

One day you wake up and realize that money makes the world go round, you need money to do basic things, so your question is, well how am I going to make some money? The way that we answer this often goes back to when you were a little kid and you were first introduced to money. Think about when you asked your parents for some money for some jeans, or to go skating, or to go buy Pokemon, or whatever it is you did when you were a kid.

To illustrate this, let me provide you with four different examples of how we think about money.

Here's how the *disempowered person* might answer that question. The disempowered person says, "I'm going to wait for the government to give me some money. I'm going to wait for the government to create opportunities for me, I'm going to wait for the government to send me a check, whatever." That's disempowerment.

It doesn't mean that you're lazy; it doesn't mean that you're bad, it just means that you don't feel that you have the ability to get it yourself—you are waiting for somebody else to give it to you. This person may rationalize that it's our government too so it's not like we don't deserve that money.

The *moderately empowered* person says, "I'm going to go get a job." Your parents might say, "Well you want some money? Boy you better go get a job." Many of us had parents like that.

Conversely, a hard working *wealth builder* takes it to the next level. She says, "Well, I don't want to go get a job, I want to create a job. I'm going to start a business." That's what a hardworking wealth builder might say.

This person acknowledges that, "No, I'm not meant to be someone's employee. You know me, for a while I was okay being the employee, but I didn't like it. I said, 'I don't think I want to be the employee, I think it's more fun to be the boss.' So how do I become the boss? How do I get his job?"

The last type of person does the least work of all; she says, "I'm going to make an investment." That's deep.

Of all the hypothetical persons addressed, the last one

recognizes that her money can make money for her.

This reminds me of a conversation I had with Dr. Claud Anderson, whom I admire and respect. He wrote two of the most important books in the history of all of black America, *Black Labor, White Wealth*, and *PowerNomics*. If your children haven't read these books, make sure your kids read these books. In fact, this should be required reading for every black family in America.

One thing Dr. Anderson said that was very insightful was, "Well, you know, actually, my Jewish friends don't really want to run a business because that's work." He said, "What they do is they will own 10% of 10 businesses, which gives you the same income as if you owned a whole business yourself, and they spend their time playing golf because they get money just by putting up the capital. Their money is working for them."

This is the fourth way that we can make money and it is an example of the expression, '*Let your money work for you.*' It is when you show up and somebody says, "Well, I want to build a bakery, and I'm ready to do the work, but I just don't have the money."

In other words, you provide the money, so you're making money just by providing the money. They're doing the actual labor. This is what I would say, in hip hop terms, is making money the fly way.

The truth is that all four options, or some combination thereof, have worked for people. If you look at wealth building historically in America, wealth has come from some government subsidies, right? So yeah, we can go and march and rally and tell President Trump or President Wilson, President Johnson, President Smith, or whoever the presidents are in the future, that we demand subsidies, right? We can tell him/her, "We want our portion. We want our reparations. We want some land. We want our homestead. We want all of that."

However, when your children are taught how to make their own money then you are teaching them how to work hard just as if they're working for someone else, but the person who they're working for is themselves. This is real power.

Most importantly, it does not have to be a white man. As this becomes more common place in our families and our communities, eventually we will graduate to a point where we build a capital base and we can reinvest that capital base in order to make ourselves wealthier.

So how do we catch up with rich folks? Well, a lot of this comes down to understanding what other people are doing, and what you're not doing, right? So we've got to readdress how we even talk about money from the very beginning. You have to let go of the idea that they have some magical voodoo or that their financial literacy is superior. Stop thinking that *they* somehow have access to a bunch of things that you'll never have access to.

Don't get me wrong, Donald Trump has exposure to things I don't and probably won't gain access to. He has access to wealthy friends I don't have. Absolutely. But there's a lot of stuff I have access to and so do you.

Remember, as I stated in Chapter 1 and its worth repeating here,—black people have more spending power than the gross domestic product of most countries on this Earth. I could go down the list from Saudi Arabia to Sweden to Venezuela to Egypt to Nigeria. There are entire countries that don't have as much money as black America has, but the thing about money is that what happens with money depends on what you can do with it.

At this point, you may be wondering, why are some people more stock market savvy than others? It is very easy to look at people who are doing something at a certain level and really attribute it all to magic. It's not magic. It's not magic.

It's very basic, and it's stuff that you've known your whole life. I just helped you understand it a little bit better. Stop believing that stock market investors are all liars and crooks or that they just have wealthy sugar daddies or mommas or somebody just gave them everything. I had none of that.

When I was 28 years old, I was homeless technically. If homeless means you have nowhere to live and you've got to leave your apartment in the middle of the night because you can't pay the rent then that was me. I had enough money to rent a one way van to Ohio because I had a place where I thought I could stay in Ohio. I had to fill that whole van up with everything I owned and leave in the middle of the night. It was not cool.

That's not fly, but it is what I felt like I had to do at that juncture in my life. So no, I probably couldn't even get a girlfriend or anything while living in a van, and it wasn't even my van.

I share this to say that I know that feeling of being empty in the bank account, but at the same time even when I had no money, I was always a billionaire because of the knowledge I was accumulating. When you know how to build things, you also know how to take things that don't have much structure to them and create what you want.

Think about it this way. If I gave you a million acres of land and you knew nothing about what to do with that land, you might think that's a waste. I could literally put you on that land and you could starve to death and be bored to death and have no income because you don't know what to do with that land.

But imagine if you had a million acres of land and the people you put on that land were carpenters and gardeners and hunters and builders and computer technicians and people who could build an electrical grid and who knew plumbing. They could make that land into a complete city.

If you had enough skill, you could literally build wealth with the skills you have. So for black folks, we must commit to excellence to the point that it becomes a consistent cultural norm. We can push the idea that all of us are capable of being wealthy in terms of our ability to use our skills to build. It's important to let that seep in.

That's why even when I was broke I still knew that I was wealthy. I had an education. When I eventually got some heart and courage to go on with my education, along with a little vision, maturity, and experience, I couldn't be stopped. So wealth building is not just not about money, it's also about motivation and tenacity.

First, you want to find out where the money is. Next, learn the system so you can decide what you want/need from the system. Furthermore, make a plan for getting access to wealth over a long period of time. That's your wealth accumulation process. This is a wealth building life cycle that I created. You might see something similar in somebody else's book somewhere I guess, but this is something I literally put together just for you. I didn't read it somewhere.

Next, it is important that you implement a long term plan. To be clear, after you learn the system, and you learn where you want to be, make a plan. After you make the plan, you implement the plan.

Implementation is a long term process of accumulating wealth over a sustained period of time. Most people don't get rich quickly, they get rich slowly.

Next, you must protect the wealth you've accumulated. Have you ever heard people say, "More money more problems?" Well, that's really true. When people get money and accumulating money is no longer a problem, your big problem, at that point, is protecting your money. Unfortunately, when you get a lot of money, everybody wants to borrow some; everybody wants to steal it from you; and everybody wants to sue you for it.

In many ways, this is also a process. You might even say that this is an animalistic concept. It is much like the way that animals kill each other in the woods to take each other's food, women, or territory.

Imagine along with me for a moment. Well, you decide to roll through the hood shining in a Mercedes with 25 gold chains around your neck with your music blasting and a pretty girl next to you because you're 2 Chainz and you're on top of the world. What's going to happen to you?

You're going to get beat up and robbed like 2 Chainz got beat up and robbed. Well, the same thing is true with rich people. If everybody knows how much you have then you're vulnerable to getting beat up and robbed. However the beating that you receive will not be physical. You will just get beat up in a legal court or somebody beats you up in the court of public opinion or whatever. Or if you're an athlete and you've got a lot of money, and you don't have any education then your manager, your lawyer, and your accountant will beat you up and rob you (I will talk about this in greater detail in another chapter).

To make it simple, at the end of the day, you want to protect the wealth that you've accumulated.

I don't know if you know this, but 70% of all wealthy families lose all their wealth within one generation. 70% to 90% lose all of their wealth within two generations. So as you accumulate wealth, start thinking about how you're going to protect it.

Also stop believing that wealth can only come to those who have money. Albert Einstein said that compound interest is the most powerful force in the universe. This is the man who created E=mc squared; he understood mysteries of the universe that no other physicists in the history of the world or mathematician had ever understood, even until this day.

He said compound interest absolutely fascinated him. Two things fascinated Einstein, from what I've read, one was compound interest, and the other one was quantum mechanics because quantum mechanics is highly nuanced. If you want to ever just see a weird horror show, go watch a video about quantum mechanics. It will freak you out.

Anyway, what does that mean when he says compound interest is the greatest force in the universe? Well, it means that money grows really quickly. Money multiplies in ways that's absolutely mind boggling. Let me show you.

Let's say you had $1,000 in principle and you let it sit. You just put your $1,000 in there and it grows.

You watch it grow. First, it grows slowly and then it starts growing a little more and a little more and a little more, and so the interest is what you earn off of the principle. The principle is what you put in the first 1,000. That doesn't change. The interest is what you're earning from the principle, but the compound interest is interest on top of interest.

I compare it to bunny rabbits. I talked about this in my investing class. Let's say your goal was to own as many rabbits as you possibly could, right? How would you accumulate a stockpile of rabbits? If they were $10 a piece, would you just go and buy 10 rabbits this week and then 10 more next week and 10 more the next week and just keep accumulating?

Then if you have $5,000 would you buy 500 rabbits at $10 a piece?

No, you don't do that. If you're smart, what you do is you buy five male rabbits and five female rabbits. You put them in a pen, you turn on some Marvin Gaye, and you let nature take its course. You let the rabbits create other rabbits. Then next thing you know, you've got rabbits on top of rabbits and then the rabbits that are born are getting together with other rabbits and making more rabbits.

Next thing you know, you've got 1,000 rabbits when you only started off with 10. Well, money grows like bunny rabbits. In a way (yes, this is the corny) think of your money as money rabbits.

Now in addition to understanding stocks and compound

interest, let's discuss annuities. Annuities are better than one lump sum of money. That $1,000 that we just showed you does grow in compound interest. Well, what if you were putting in $1,000 a year? Or $1,000 a month.

And you had this same process occurring, except it's occurring hundreds of times because over many, many years you're just doing it every single month. Well, that's what an annuity is. An annuity is when you're putting the same amount of money in every single time. Just like your $5 a day. Just imagine doing it over and over and over again.

Many people receive annuities if they come into a large sum of money—this can be the result of a legal payout or a lawsuit. Often the method of distribution is determined by the person. Whatever is chosen allows both your principle and interest to grow together. So you're putting your money in, the money earns interest, the interest earns more interest, but then you're putting in more money which is earning more interest which is earning more compound interest. This accelerates the process.

What happens is you create power. This creates financial power. When I first started sharing this information, I had a real hard time trying to convince black people that we can actually do something. We can actually build something because there's so many people who really believe that we're just broke and that's where we're supposed to be forever and it bothers me very much. So I sat around thinking about creative ways to help people understand how anybody, historically anyway, can build wealth if that's what they choose to do.

This is why $5 is my magic number. If you go to a coffee shop and you get a water and a banana, you're going to spend more than $5. If you get a large coffee and a muffin, you're going to spend about seven, eight, nine dollars or more.

So the $5 a day investment plan is less than the cost that it takes to go to Starbucks, or even to go to McDonald's and order off of the dollar menu. You can't even buy that much gas for $5. Let's say you earn $10 an hour. Most of us make more than that, but those of you who make $10 an hour can even get with this plan as well. You work 40 hours a week, so that's $80 a day. You're earning $400 a week or $1,600 a month.

Now, let's assume that $5 a day is lunch money, right? So you can get an app like coin stash or robin hood and invest $5 a day in what auto stash.

The question is how much money would you have after 10 years? Remember, you're broke, you don't have anything. You are flat broke. You're like me when I was in my van moving in the middle of the night with my basketball on the dashboard because I had all of my stuff in the back of the van. You don't have anything, so you're not starting from anything. How much money would you have after 10 years?

Well, after 10 years if you don't save at all, you'll have nothing to show for it, so imagine if you just saved that money instead of spending it. Start small if you have to so that you can have a benchmark.

Let's say that you are not comfortable with any of this just yet. Don't worry. We can examine how to make your savings account work for you.

Okay, so if you started poor, you'll finish poor. That's what some people believe, that's what you're taught in America. If you're born poor then there's nothing you can do about it. You're kind of trained to be hopeless and helpless. I know this isn't true Well, everyone can open a savings account.

My grandmother was a saver. My grandmother used to save—that's all she did. She didn't invest anything because she didn't want to lose her money. So you save your money so you have $150 in a month, approximately, assuming a 30 day month, which approximately is about $1,800 a year, which over a decade is about $18,000. Over 20 years, it's $36,000, and over 30 years that's $54,000.

So that's not bad, right? I mean if you save $5 a day for 30 years then you've got 54k; you're not poor. You're no longer in poverty. I mean, you're not balling, but you're not destitute, right? So saving isn't a horrible way to build money, but here's the thing.

A savings account can give you financial security and an insulator from poverty, but it doesn't actually give you a chance to move up. We want to do the George and Wheezy; we want to move on up. We don't want to sit still. So let's talk about how you can move on up. The problem with saving is that your money doesn't grow, so this keeps you from enjoying the benefits of living in a money and capital driven society.

You see, when you live in a society where there's investment opportunities everywhere, businesses starting everywhere, and people looking for capital everywhere, you shouldn't sit on the $54,000 that you have saved up. It is equivalent to having the nicest car in the world in your garage and you're not even driving it. You're not driving it. No one can rent it and no one can get in it because you don't want to get the seats dirty, right? You don't want anyone to wreck your car. Well, that's a problem.

Many black people don't invest because they're afraid. Thankfully, there are ways to overcome all of that. A lot of this fear is totally unfounded. There are complete theories I can show you that will say that if you allowed fear to keep you out of the stock market then you have missed out on a great opportunity for no good reason. Let me dig a little deeper.

All right, so imagine if you invested that $5 a day instead of sitting on it. Let's say that instead of saving it, you actually took it and you said, "Let me let this money work for me." Let's assume you earn 9% per year on your investments on what they call a diversified portfolio, which means that you don't put all of your eggs in one basket. 9% a year is a reasonable assumption based on what the market has done up until this point.

How much would you have after 10 years? Well, remember, before you had 18,000 after 10 years. Now look at what you have after 10 years. We have three levels here. We have no savings. This is what happens when you go spend your money on Gucci belts and sneakers and t-shirts and trying to be fly. You're down here at the zero mark. You're just over broke and you've got to keep working because you have no backup plan. You're playing strugglenomics right here.

Now, if you're a saver; you're smart. You're smart, but you're a wimp, so your money hasn't actually grown, but you've been accumulating so good for you. That's good. Now, past performance does not always predict future performance, but the investor would do better than the person who simply saved.

At the 20 year mark, the saver has accumulated about $36,000, but the investor has over $102,000. Now let's think about 30 years. The saver has accumulated $54,000, but the investor has about $281,000.

Given that this person started off working for $10 an hour and committed to investing $5 a day, there's no way on Earth that this person, who has $281,000 in liquid financial assets, could call himself poor or financially unstable anymore. In fact, he isn't poor after the 10 year mark. He's actually ascended to the top 5% of Americans.

Now let's think about the 40 year mark. What if you did that for 40 years? What if you went out 40 years and you did the same strategy? This number is over $700,000. Now, 40 years is a long time, that's about the average working life of a 25 year old. That means that person would be able to leave three quarters of a million dollars to their family. It means that if you had a child, and you started a $5 a day investment plan for your newborn baby, by the time your child turns 40, based on history, your child would have hundreds of thousands of dollars in assets to play with.

When your child, 40 years from now, is competing with Barron Trump—Donald Trump's son, who he's preparing to be a boss, not to be anybody's employee—the question is whether or not your child can stand up to Barron Trump? What playing field did you set up for him. Did you lay out a foundation for him or did you leave him hanging out to dry?

Dr. Claud Anderson said that it's criminal to send your child to somebody who hates him to go beg for a job because he can't pay his own bills and can't feed his own family. It's criminal. So it's absolutely criminal, in my opinion, for you not to invest for your child and for you not to teach your child how to compete in a competitive, economic society.

It is unfortunate, but true that Black people were never taught how to compete. It is not your fault. If you go read *Black Labor, White Wealth*, one of Dr. Anderson's best books, he quotes 19th century laws put in place that stated that the goal for black people was to make them into a reliable, hardworking, well-disciplined, uncompetitive and subordinated labor force. If you're not competitive, it isn't your fault. You were trained to be that way, but it's time for that jig to be up. It's time to end that right now.

You can compete even if you're starting off at the bottom. Here's what I want you to remember, number one, the differences between saving and investing. They grow at what you call a non-linear rate. That means that as more time goes by, the more the gap increases, so it becomes that much more pronounced, or that much more dramatic.

When you are an investor, your number one asset is not money, your number one asset is time. A person with no money and a lot of time is better off than a person with a lot of money and no time. Period. If you're reading and you're in your 20s, you are better off than a millionaire in their 50s. That is a mathematical fact. The question is, what are you going to do with this precious commodity called time?

Are you going to waste it or are you going to invest it? If you are sitting around feeling sorry for yourself then you're wasting it. If you're hustling and making moves and making things happen, getting knowledge, investing and putting things together, and/or building your portfolio, then you're investing that time properly. You will end the game ahead.

Next, a person who starts poor doesn't have to remain that way. I don't care what anybody tells you, I just showed you mathematically that a person, with some discipline, who has a low income (makes a little above minimum wage) can actually build something. A poor person who wants their child to be well off has a clear pathway to get their child out of poverty.

If you can't get yourself out, if you can't do right by you, do right by your babies anyway. Please. My goodness. No, it's not magic; it's math. That's all it is; it's basic math. If it's math that confuses you a little bit or boggles you or makes you feel uncomfortable, don't feel bad because Albert Einstein felt the same way. It boggled him. It made him think, "This can't be right. There's no way money can grow this fast."

It can and believe it or not, it doesn't matter what stock you start with. A lot of people think that it is complicated to pick stocks, it's really not. I point you guys to the book called *A Random Walk Down Wall Street* by Burton Malkiel. In that book, he does an experiment where he has monkeys pick stocks, and basically the monkeys actually make more money than the experts from Wall Street and the reason is because monkeys don't make it complicated. The monkeys would just pick the stock and go eat bananas or whatever and let the stocks grow. Basically, he showed his readers that if you just diversify, you're usually going to be in good shape. What you don't want to do is not diversify.

To do this, I recommend that you diversify and make sure to

keep it as liquid as you need to keep it. For example, a liquid investment is like a stock, because you can buy stocks pretty easily. An illiquid investment is like art. Art is hard to sell. Stocks are very easy to sell. So keep it liquid; keep it diversified, and keep it consistent.

Remember that time is literally more valuable than money in investing. Use your time to your benefit. Don't waste time. When you waste time, you really are wasting an unbelievable amount of money.

So investing is a lot like picking clothes. It's like one's style. Maybe you like jeans and I like something else, corduroy or something. Does anybody wear corduroy anymore or did I just sound really old when I wrote that? Remember, the world is changing. You can reshape your paradigm and your approach based on the existing opportunities that are out there or you can stay locked in the past which means that several opportunities will elude you. You can't live in 2017 with a 1992 mindset; that's not going to work. It's just not going to work for you.

Think of it this way. Anything that you can predict based on information, can be looked up in a magazine or a book. Remember that millions of other people have that same information. Because of this, prices change based on the information.

Let's say, for example, there's information in *Time Magazine* that says that General Electric is going to make an extra $10 billion a year next year, and you say, "Oh my God, I just read that GE is going to be making all this money. I'm going to go buy some GE stock."

Well, by the time you go back and buy it, the price would have already changed to reflect that information. Investors would have already pushed the price up. So you're paying more for that company because it's a more valuable company because of this information that's been released. That's what they call the efficient markets hypothesis, which leads to what they call the random walk theory in finance.

I won't go into either of these in greater detail because my goal is to guide you in a way that's going to make sense. I just wanted you be aware of those terms in case you decide to do further research. In fact, I created *theblackstockmarketprogram.com* to address questions that I cannot cover in this chapter or book.

As you reflect back over the information that I shared in this chapter, I want you to think about your current relationship with money. What should you do differently? And how will your decisions determine your children's relationship with money?

CHAPTER 3

HOW TO AVOID GOING FOR BROKE: THE VIN BAKER STORY

In the previous two chapters, I have discussed how to obtain wealth and the role that saving, being fiscally responsible, and investing in the stock market can all play in growing your money. Just as there are examples of people who have excelled. There are also cautionary tales that we can learn from. The focus of this chapter is not to blame a person, but rather to look at some of the steps that were taken and choices that were made that led a multi-millionaire down the path of financial ruin.

Vinn Baker was a beloved basketball start. He demonstrated great athleticism and basketball prowess. He showed promise early on and basketball served as a catapult for his entry into the millionaire's club. If one is not careful, what goes up will eventually come down.

You are probably familiar with the story of former NBA player Vin Baker. Vin was a very good player when he played in the NBA. He made the All-Star Team four times. He was off the chain in terms of his athletic ability. Unfortunately, his money management skills left a few things to be desired. He ended up going broke. He's now working at the local Starbucks up in his hometown of in Rhode Island.

This story is obviously sad and heartbreaking. I remember when Vin was in the NBA. I remember that he had trouble with alcohol, and he also struggled a little bit in the league in terms of personal decisions, but I also remember that throughout the course of his career, he made a lot of money. In fact, he made a $100 million. That's a lot of money to make over a short period of time and still go broke.

Vin's story reminds us all that even though other people might be out to exploit us, we often co-sign our own exploitation. In other words, to use a basketball metaphor, exploitation requires some degree of teamwork between you and the person that is exploiting you.

Of course, I have concerns about Vin as a black man. I didn't understand why the former Starbucks CEO helped Vin out by letting him work in a local Starbucks, but he didn't help him out by putting him in the front office of an NBA team or letting him do something that would allow him to generate an income while also preserving his dignity.

Now, here's what I want to discuss in terms of the sheer absurdity of Vin making this kind of money and going broke. $100 million dollars—just think about that about in real terms. Having that kind of money go out of your hands is a financial tragedy of epic proportions and I don't care who you are. That's the kind of money that shouldn't just take care of you for the rest of your life. It is the kind of money that should take care of you, everybody you love, and everybody they love and everybody they give birth to and their great-grandchildren, great-grandchildren, great-great grandchildren for the next 300 years. You understand?

If wealth is managed properly, wealth is capital. Capital is supposed to grow in value over time. That's why when you see very wealthy families, they are extremely careful about making sure that each generation understands the value of the capital, how to manage the capital, and how to be responsible with the capital. They have a team of financial advisers. They have trust funds set up to protect the wealth so that one person can't just blow it all and screw everything up for the family. You understand?

When you really think about what happened here, this isn't just a tragedy for Vin Baker. This is a tragedy for his children, his grandchildren, and his great-grandchildren. All of whom could have benefited from this money because when you get money of that magnitude that money is supposed to work for you. It's almost like having a team of employees that are all out hustling for you—there only job is to bring in money for you.

I'll give you a good example. Mark Zuckerberg is worth far more than $100 million. He's worth about $34 billion. A lot of people don't understand this, but Mark Zuckerberg, by not even working, but allowing his money to work for him, makes more money in about four days than LeBron James makes in an entire season. He'll make more money in about four months than LeBron James will make in his entire career.

The fact is that financial irresponsibility or this kind of financial craziness should bother everybody because you have to work really, really hard to waste $100 million. You've just got to be beyond financially sloppy. You have to be financially self-destructive. It's most like finding a way to chop a rock in little pieces. You have to hammer extremely hard to break that rock into little pieces because that rock is not meant to be chopped up like that. $100 million is not meant to be wasted. It's very hard to do that even if you live an opulent, flashy, materialistic or over-the-top life.

Let me just give you a quick layout in terms of a very simple approach. This is not rocket science. I'm not going to lay out any heavy financial concepts to you. Instead, I'm going to give you a very simple way that we can guarantee that no NBA player, or anyone else reading this book, would ever have to go broke even if they spent money like an idiot.

Imagine that you have an NBA player who is going to make $8 million dollars a year. Let's assume his career is going to be 10 years. $8 million is not on the low end of NBA salaries, but it's not on the high end either. There are guys that make a whole lot more money, especially when you throw in endorsements and all of these other opportunities that come with being a person of that stature at that income level. Not only are you making a lot of money from your team, but you should be at some point getting endorsements and monetizing your brand.

You should also, at some point, have investments that are making money for you. You should have relationships with other people who will allow you to make more money. Money should breed more money. It shouldn't just be a matter of me just getting a little paycheck from the man and being a high paid employee, and then going broke as soon as the man stops sending me money. That's not how money is supposed to work. A good financial adviser will tell you that.

Imagine that this player makes $8 million a year. Okay, cool. You're making $8 million a year. It's about $666,000 a month. Now, let's assume that this player just saves 10% of that income. I know that that's pre-tax income and taxes are going to chip away at that. If they take out the bottom 10% and they put aside $67,000 a month, it would still leave them about $600,000 a month. Suddenly, all of these little vultures and leeches and all these other people start coming out and taking the player's money.

These Harvard educated agents, managers, and attorneys are all waiting for these young brothers to come into the league to make all of this money so that they can find a way to exploit them, (it's not a coincidence that many of our most prominent, most capable black athletes are left severely uneducated). It is just a matter of time before a fool and his money will always part ways.

Never ever be a fool.

The most valuable thing a black man can have in America is his education. Don't let anybody tell you anything different. All these vultures come along. The vultures take their cut. Let's say that after the vultures take their cut, there's $350 left. You take out 66 of the top, so you got between a quarter million to $300,000 a month. Let's think about that. It's a quarter of a million dollars a month that you have and can do whatever you want with it.

You go to the club, throw it in the air and you can make it rain. You go buy a Bentley. You can get your garage full of stupid cars and spending money on Gucci and Prada and all of these other European brands that don't want to hire black people. You can do all of that stupid stuff you want. You can just be an absolute fool with the rest of your money, but you must put aside the $67,000 a month. You put it into an investment portfolio.

Now, let's say that you do that consistently. You go to your mama or you go to somebody who you trust like your uncle Willy, your sister or your investment adviser and say, "Look, every month you're going to take $67,000 or 10% of my income out of my check. I can't touch it. You have legal rights to that money. I have to pay you like a bill. You are my first bill that I get before I get a mortgage, a car note, and all the other things that might leave broke." That's your first bill, $67,000 a month goes into an earmarked account.

Now, they take this money and they put it into a mutual fund that has average risk level for the stock market. They'll know what to do. Good financial advisers will know how to put your money into a diversified portfolio, a mutual fund, something like that. Just tell them to do that. Tell them to read this book if you're an NBA player or an NBA player's mama or somebody who wants the best for her child. Put the money in a diversified portfolio with an average risk level that matches that of the stock market.

Let's assume that over the decade that that player's in the NBA. he has a reasonably healthy career, but not too long. Right? 10 years. 10 years is not quite a really long career, but it's not a short career either.

He does 10 years in the NBA and makes $8 million a year. He doesn't get any pay raises, which is another very conservative assumption, because he should get a salary increase. Over 10 years, he makes $80 million total. $67,000 is being put into that account *every* month faithfully. It's being invested in the portfolio and growing over time. Let me tell you about the magic of compound interest.

You see, if you ask most people how much money will he have if he invests $67,000 a month over 10 straight years will simply multiply it by 120 months. They're going to say, "Oh yeah, man. You have $8 million. That's amazing."

However, what they're not factoring in is the power of compound interest that I discussed in Chapter 2.

The fact that money grows on top of money which grows on top of money is like the way a virus grows—this might work better for those of you who did not like my money rabbit metaphor.

You ever think about a virus? A virus can be spread amongst four people, but then those four people might each infect four more people, and then those four people may infect four additional people. The next thing you know, a 100 million people have the same virus that started with four people.

Money grows like that. Money grows in a very natural viral

sense. That's why a lot of our financial equations that we studied in school are built actually on biology and the way things grow in nature. Money grows in top of money, so actually instead of that $67,000 a month growing into $8 million, that's $67,000 a month will grow into over $12 million at an 8% rate of return.

Now, if he's able to get a higher rate of return, which actually is not that hard to do; I usually get about 30% to 40% a year on my investments because I invest in dot-coms, and I invest in companies where I see opportunities to flip money and make big money really fast. If you're a smart investor, you can make 20%, 30%, 40%, 50% a year on your money. I have put $5,000 into businesses that have made me a quarter million dollars in two years.

There's ways to make more, but let's assume that you're very conservative. You're only making about 8% on your money. You would have $12 million by the time you're done. Now, $12 million is enough money for you to live off for the rest of your life. That's the kind of money that you could put in a trust fund and give yourself a nice salary.

Give yourself half a million dollars a year, $700,00 or whatever works best for you. Add that to your NBA pension on top of that, and you can still live like a baller for the rest of your life. You don't have to go broke just because you want to spend a little bit of money. That's the thing that most people don't understand. You don't have to live frugally, you have to live responsibly.

In other words, you don't have to be financially frugal and prudent in order to build wealth. You don't have to do that. You just have to have balance. You have to be determined not to throw all of your money away.

Honestly, that's one of the things that I don't understand. I really wish that there was some mechanism where these guys could really get the kind of advice they need to get because whoever is advising these guys is screwing them. A lot of these people will take their little fee off of the top, and they don't care what happens to your black butt once your NBA career is over.

They're going to take their money. They're going to take that money. They're going to build wealth for their family. They're going to build generational wealth. They're sending their kids to elite private schools, buying them BMWs, and paying for Harvard.

They're making sure their daughter has her wedding paid for. They're making sure their son has his first down payment on a house.

They're making sure their kids aren't going to have to go $100,000 in debt to go to college. They're making sure that each generation in their family is not starting over. When you look at Vin Baker, the tragedy here is that his children and his grandchildren and his great-grandchildren will have to start over. That is sick. That is sad.

I'm very sorry that the brother had a substance abuse problem. This is another way to lose a whole lot of money. That's why I suggest every black man in America should say no to drugs and alcohol. Tell your children, say no to it. We live in a country that encourages you to use drugs. A lot of the biggest drug dealers are actually legalized pharmaceutical companies.

Don't buy into the idea that alcohol is benign. Alcohol is a deep part of American culture. In 1836 the average American drank the equivalent of about 83 bottles of whiskey every year. America is a country of drunks. They make a lot of money by making you think that alcohol is safe, when actually alcohol destroys a lot of lives. Vin Baker is a great example of that. He talks openly and regularly about his alcohol addiction and what it did to him and how it destroyed his life.

Long story short, when you get this money, just be smart. You don't have to be a financial wizard. You don't have to be cheap or incredibly frugal with you money. You also don't have to work so hard that you destroy your wealth because when you make that kind of money and you throw that money away, you're not just hurting yourself. You're hurting everybody who loves you. You're hurting everybody who could have benefited from your choices.

You're hurting all of the thousands of children you could have educated by building a school. You're hurting all of the hundreds of families you could have helped by building a business or building an institution that would employ black people. You're hurting all of your descendants who could have benefited from the massive amount of wealth that you could have built during your lifetime.

It isn't just about just you, Vin, or someone else throwing away one's money and life. That's truly sad. That's a tragedy, absolutely. It's about all the people who were affected.

When I created the business school, I wanted to provide people with options that would allow them to carve out their own financial freedom. We all have different gifts, so the paths that we take are as diverse as we are. What I hope is that we will not continue to hear Vin Baker-like stories or about young men and women who are ill equipped to handle and protect their finances.

The Black Wealth Bootcamp provides me and my fellow instructors with a platform that will empower you. Perhaps if Vin had people in his corner who poured into his life instead of draining it, this cautionary tale would be non-existent. Sadly, it is not. And, there are so many others who have experienced a similar fate. The point is that we can do something about it. We have to do something about it.

CHAPTER 4

FIGHT THE POWER: ARE WE GOING ABOUT IT THE WRONG WAY?

If you watch the news then you are sure to walk away with the idea that Black folks are in trouble. However, I don't subscribe to that at all. In fact, I think that at this very moment, we are positioned to excel in ways that we have never exceled before and it all goes back to black American money.

Sure marches and protests have their place, but what happens in those neighborhoods after the cameras leave and national attention moves on to a new city? Are there more jobs? More opportunities?

There is nothing wrong with fighting the power. The real question is how?

Let's look at HBCUs as an example of how power brokering often plays out in America. One of the things that always affected me and bothered me is the fact that a lot of these schools have great difficulty recruiting and retaining black faculty members.

Paradoxically, a lot of the professors are not black. In all of the years that I spent in school, and believe me I spent a lot of years in school—I went through four years of college and I was in graduate school for another nine years getting several master's degrees in math, and statistics—I didn't have one single black professor, not one, not one.

I thought that was kind of unusual, but actually, that's pretty common in a lot of American business schools and it's even becoming true in a lot of HBCU's, especially if you major in business or in the sciences. If you went to an HBCU, go back and ask yourself, how many African American professors, not just black, did you see teaching in the business school? How many did you see teaching in the school of computer science, engineering, etc.? You'll find that the numbers are low.

This led me to say, "Okay, something needs to give, something needs to change." Another thing that has always bothered me about college is that the world is changing and some universities are changing with the world, some of them are not, but one of the things that many universities are doing quite consistently and across the board is leaving students saddled with a lifetime amount of crippling debt.

This means that you're 22 years old and you've already got a mortgage. You probably won't be able to get a house of your own because you're already paying a mortgage called student loans. Then on top of that, you're jumping into an economic system that's not what it used to be.

Now there's money being made, perhaps trillions of dollars, not billions, trillions of dollars being made on the internet, through business development, and e-commerce. The problem is that a lot of universities are not teaching students, and black students in particular, how to benefit from these trends. If they are being taught this information, they're not being taught by people who actually know how to do it. Instead, their instructors are often people who make their money just by teaching other people how to make money. That's not a legitimate way to teach people if you ask me.

I remember thinking to myself, "There's got to be a better way, to get away from this massive debt, this outdated information and this environment that's not culturally relevant for black people." Also, I wanted to deal with the fact that when black people come out of these universities, we still have the highest unemployment rate in the country. A black college graduate in many cases has a lower likelihood of getting a job than a white man with a high school diploma and sometimes even less likely than a white man with a criminal record.

What does that mean? Well that means that we've got to do things different. If we want real change, we can't just march and we can't just protest. We have to change the life trajectories of black people. We have to get our education in our way and on our own terms with a new framework.

We must educate ourselves. The Black Business School is a model of what this can look like. Number one, everything's black. I mean, the word black is in the title. We don't hide from the word black, we don't use multicultural, and minority, and diverse. No, we're talking about black people and we're talking about black people getting a head. We're talking about black wealth that matters, black people that matters, black families that matter, the black community that matters.

It is worth noting that people will sometimes ask me why I often place the word black in my titles, on my platforms, and in my videos. I like using the word black because I get tired of people being scared of being black and being afraid to say the word black or pretend that blackness should always be an afterthought. I don't think blackness should be an afterthought, blackness should be the preliminary thought.

I can't see anything without seeing it through the lens of blackness, and I choose to be that way because that's what we need. My energy's best applied when it's directed to the community. I'm not trying to apply it to everybody and let black people kind of tag along.

Black, black, black, black, black. We're not afraid to say that; we're not afraid to be black; we're not afraid to represent you and we are committed to putting people in front of you who are knowledgeable about their topics and who love black people. No disrespect to white institutions and learning platforms, but we're trying to keep things very authentic, or as some people might say, we are "keeping it real" because we care deeply about our community; we have the credentials, and the expertise to facilitate success.

One of the ways that Black people are not presented with opportunities to advance is that an education is often cost prohibitive. When things are not affordable, we tend to shy away from them or see ourselves as being excluded from them. My intent in making the Black Business School affordable is that I wanted people, regardless of their current financial situation, to have access to classes and not walk away with debt.

You'll have at least 10, 20, 50,000 in debt at most universities. In the Black Business School, you'll have no debt. You're not giving up on quality because I have a real Ph.D., I have friends and colleagues who have earned Ph.D.'s who have agreed to come in and support you and teach you. Also, they're not muddled down with bureaucracy. They can teach you outside the lines and they can do whatever is necessary to help you become successful.

We will meet in a virtual classroom and I'm going to give you a lesson, give you knowledge and information, but I'm not going to do what people might do in a college campus which is send you away and say, "Okay, learn the rest of this stuff in your dorm room. Good luck. That's on you."

No, I will support you. I will track you. If you're trying to start a business, then tell me about your business, let me know how it works. If you're looking for a mentor, well I'm here forever. It doesn't end when the class ends, it doesn't end when you're four years in college ends. It can go on forever. I have students that have worked with me for several years and I've mentored them all along the way.

Then finally, maybe I'll partner with you. I mean, if you have a business and you're looking for partners or you're looking for an affiliate, I'll sign up if it's something that fits for my audience. I will be more than happy to tell people about your product, and help you get your business off the ground, or help you really get that in-between-the-lines information that will help you launch or accelerate your business.

Because here's the thing, the Black Business School's primary ideology is built on the idea of black people building things and owning things. We don't borrow power. You don't beg for power nor should you think that you should ever have to. You don't accumulate true and meaningful power by aligning yourself with somebody else's institution. That's just not going to work.

You fight the power by being empowered.

In the Black Business School, our goal is to teach you how to build, to teach you how to own, to teach you how to grow something that is yours, and to give you something that's a meaningful, culturally relevant, empowered experience without all the bureaucracy. We can do whatever we want; we can say what we want; and we can even cuss if we want to. It doesn't matter, whatever it takes to get the job done, that's what we're here to do.

If we are serious about creating economic viability in our communities then we must also be serious about providing people with the opportunities to own. If you don't know the rules of engagement then how can you play the game? Basically, we carry you all the way through the process.

I'm putting something in front of you that's real; that's powerful; and that's going to help you. It's revolutionary; it's innovative, and it is built for the 21st Century. Because here's the thing, if black people continue to try to do things the same old-fashioned way, we're going to get the same old results.

If we keep giving $150,000.00 to these big universities then they're going to keep getting rich while we keep on struggling. If we keep going out into this economy that was built for people who are not black then we're going to keep on being frustrated because we're not the ones getting the jobs; we're not the ones getting the raises and promotions; and we're the ones being laid off first and disrespected at the end of the day because we don't own something that's ours.

Black American money is all about creating, building and sustaining wealth in our communities—that is truly fighting the power.

CHAPTER 5

YES, OUR CHILDREN ARE WATCHING

What does your relationship with money tell your children about its value? It is a simple question that may be difficult to answer, but the reality is that children emulate what they see.

Life is too short to be ignorant, so let's read books. Let's just become ferociously educated, ferociously aware and focused. As our children are learning their core subjects, we must also teach them about financial literacy.

When we created the financial literacy flashcards, for example, I wanted us to have an easy, readily accessible, and tangible way to introduce our children to money. If we position our children to see themselves as owners early on then we can have a community where the majority of our children know basic financial literacy at a reasonably high level at an early age.

Studying financial literacy can be a daily practice. You have time after school or on the weekends. Why not train your child and give them something? I swear to God if you give it to them now, it's going to be with them in 50 years. I kid you not. I swear. I put it on my grandmamma, and you all know how much I love my grandmamma.

Every child should be exposed to concepts like wealth and mutual funds. What is a mutual fund? Then there's taxes. You should even introduce them to the concept of stocks early on. I like for black people, black children, to see black people building wealth because I want them to associate wealth with blackness, not just balling and throwing money away at the club. I want them to see wealth accumulation as part of blackness.

Somebody once said, "They can learn to dab. They can learn your flashcards." Absolutely. I'm an expert at finance, but I don't know how to dab. Interestingly, the last time I checked, dabbing hasn't paid a bill up in my house, so I am not trying to learn how to dab. I'm trying to learn how to dab in this dollar bill so I can build for my family and leave something for my community and develop something of strength in a competitive world.

Here is our leverage. A lot of people don't really, can't really define exactly what financial leverage is, but I can explain it to your child literally in 30 seconds. Imagine that your child is going to school and your child knows what an asset class is. They know what mortgages are. They know what inflation is. They know what an ROI, return on investment, is. They know what equity is.

How many kids know what equity is? Most kids don't know what equity is, but they know what it means to go the mall and buy some sneakers, or a new coat, or some Beats by Dre headphones. They know how to do that.

They also need to know the value of uplifting each other. A lot of people will start off working with the black community, but then somebody else will come along and say, "You know you could make a lot more money if you did stuff for white folks." When people say that to me, I'm like, "No, no, no. I'm black. I ain't going to change that, and I work for black people."

When we put the same energy and effort in teaching our

children how to respect money and how to save money as we do with teaching them how to sing and how to dance, we will begin to help them prioritize. There is nothing wrong with wanting to be the next Beyonce, but wouldn't it be even better if you own the stadiums that Beyonce performs in? Where is the real power?

Fame is manufactured and it tends to draw our children in. They see it and they want it. What they don't often see is the process or work that was required to be successful. By demystifying financial literacy, children will not only understand, but apply this knowledge as they matriculate through school.

This work is so critical to our survival that Rev. Dr. Kevin Cosby, the president of Simmons College and the pastor at the largest mega church in the state of Kentucky, St. Stephen Church in Louisville, talks about the torch that has been passed down to us by our forefathers. I love what the brother does because when we talk, we have great conversations. He has introduced me to things that I didn't know. We talk about issues in a way that convinces me that I am not alone in my mission of ongoing black institution building.

One of the things that we had discussed was a book called *Men of Mark*. The book is an exploration of great Black men who changed the world as we know it. It was written in the 19th century, over 100 years ago, and it was written by black people who had just left the plantation and who were building for their children and future generations.

They were not sitting on one $1.1 trillion talking about, "We's broke, Massa. We can't do nuttin' for ourselves." They weren't doing any of that. They were literally like, "At least we're free, which makes us wealthy. We're wealthy because we're free and we're smart," and they started building with what they had.

They built Simmons College over 100 years ago, which is the 107th HBCU in this country because they said, "We don't need much, but we just need some books, and we need some teachers, and we need some buildings, and we're going to educate our own people because we ain't waiting on white folks to do it for us. White people ain't going to do it for us."

They built this institution. They educated thousands of black people, and the school fell into disrepair. Why did it fall into disrepair? Because of integration and because we, collectively, decided, "Hey, I want to, but the white man's ice is so much colder. This ice is cold, but the white man, I mean, his ice is really cold." They ran across town, and nobody wanted to be affiliated with the black school anymore, so they went off and hung out with the white folks, and the school, built by former slaves, was closed.

Pastor Cosby got his church to get behind him to go buy the buildings and to rejuvenate this school. He got it accredited and reopened the school so that the school's mission of service could live on.

With our own infrastructures, we really have the ingredients to resurrect Black Wall Street." We have a film called *Resurrecting Black Wall Street* and it's not a coincidence that I'm really feeling like, "Okay, wait. You know what? Now, I think I see the essence of what we were talking about in this film two years ago."

I think we can rebuild the spirit of Black Wall Street. When we bring together our common spirit of upliftment, which we all have, we set the tone for our children. We show them by our actions what it means to be members of our communities.

In fact, there are so many woke black people right now. I'm using that slang term "woke." People talk about, "Are you woke?" Yeah, man. I mean, it's beautiful. Even ignorant people are woke now.

No harm intended, but even ignorant people know that they're ignorant now. That's the first step towards a revelation—helping people understand just how messed up their thinking already is. If I could sit down with a Rich Homie Quan, or a Young Thug, or others like that, and help them understand why representation matters and that they're being ignorant, that would be a beautiful, beautiful day.

We're starting to wake up as black people and we're finally finding out and embracing who we are. We're starting to figure out how to bring together our collective power. All of these resources and all of this energy that's out here is sort of being pulled together in one pile. Then you sprinkle some money in there, strategically invested money, and you can grow something extraordinary. The thing about black people that you have to understand is this: We are some of the baddest people on this earth.

We are the baddest. There's nobody else. And yes, I know that baddest is not a word—that is just how bad we are, we had to make up a word to describe us.

They say this, in so many words, in the book *Men of Mark*. Pastor Cosby references this often, so I'm paraphrasing what he has said. He asks what other group of people do you know who can go through the worst form of slavery known to man, who can go through the Middle Passage, who can endure hundreds of years of dehumanization, rape, murder, castration, domestic terrorism, legalized oppression and still decades later produce doctors and lawyers and professors?

Let that sink in.

When other groups get hammered like that, they don't survive. Look at what happened to the Native Americans, for example. Look at what they went through and what happened to them. I am not disrespecting them or their culture, but I'm saying that their response was more natural, I think. Most people would be decimated after going through what they went through, but we just 'take a lickin' and keep on tickin'.

The only people capable of killing black people are black people. We're the only ones strong enough to prevent our own advancement, our own growth, our own development.

When people say that there really is some kind of magic in the melanin, this is not an overreach. There's a magic in the melanin. You really have a right to be proud because when you put your mind to something, you really cannot be stopped. When we, as a collective, decide that we're going to do something, we can't be stopped.

In many ways, we then live forever—not literally, but symbolically.

How do I know I'm going to live forever? Because I know that the education, knowledge, and ideas that I'm sharing with you are so powerful that these ideas cannot die, that you cannot walk away from learning this information and not go tell your friends about it, or not talk to your kids about it.

There's no way, no way. I designed it that way. I set it up that way. I set it up to not be an average dude. When I meet people around the country, they don't just say, "Oh yeah, I saw you on TV. I like you, but ..." I don't care about people seeing me on CNN. I don't care about somebody just knowing my name.

I remember once when I had a conversation like this with Dr.

Marc Lamont Hill back when we were really good friends, back in the day. We've had some disagreements since then, but I still love him because life is too short to be running around being mad at people.

In 2007, when we were talking about careers and trying to figure out how to make certain things happen, I remember saying to him, "I don't really care if people like me or don't like me." I said, "I also don't really care if they know me or don't know me, but if you know me, whether you like me or don't like me, you're going to know what I stand for. I will not be ambiguous. You are not going to wonder where I stand on important issues especially as it related to race, and I'm willing to take whatever comes with that."

What that means to me, and why it matters to you, is that my goal was to make sure that if I share something with you that I do so with great intention and purpose. Why am I talking to you if I can't give you something that's going to affect your life in a meaningful way? Why would I want to be famous just because I can tell funny jokes on my Facebook page or I can take hundreds of selfies on Instagram? Better yet, what is the point if I tell you about some stupid movie I'm going to be in that you're going to forget about by next year?

To me, these activities are not meaningful. It is not a productive use of fame and power. Fame and power, in my opinion, should be utilized to educate and strengthen and elevate the masses. That's what we all have to do.

It starts with the simple things. Things like home libraries with black books, signage with black images, and resources for black people in your home that send a message to those who are following us, especially our children. You don't have to be an art collector and you don't have to spend a lot of money to do this, you can even use a calendar to reiterate the importance of black culture and black wealth. For example, the Black Wealth calendar was designed to make wealth a normal part of your day-to-day life.

When you see it every day on the refrigerator, it serves as a reminder of the various ways that we can implement wealth-building, entrepreneurship, cooperative economics, and institution building. Each month has a theme. One month is debt reduction month. Another month is home ownership month. A different month is entrepreneurship month. And yet another month is savings and budgeting month.

These things are not by default, they come about due to our consistent daily habits. It's all about the habits. The devil is in the details. That's what holds us back is that we don't have the habits to become who we want to be.

Ultimately the goal is to make it part of the culture. I want wealth-building, and I want entrepreneurship, and I want economic empowerment to be as fundamental to who we are as going to church. I really want that to be the new gospel for black people. I kid you not.

Realistically, sometimes what you say you want to be doesn't match what your subconscious is telling you to be because you spend so many years being brainwashed to believe that you're supposed to be lazy and complacent. The only time you get excited is when it's time to stand up and do the Electric Slide, but actually you should be just as excited when it's time to stand up and build something with your people.

Our goal is to be a little bit like a church in the sense that a church's main mission should be to be there for the people—not the pastor. A good church is there for everybody. It's like saying, "Okay, we got the gym over here for the kids. We got the daycare for your children. We got Sunday school. We got this reading class. We got a class on mortgages." The church meets the needs of the people in their totality.

Metaphorically, that's what we do. What we have in place with the Black Business School are resources that help you to build and to grow. When students, for example, go through the Black Wealth Bootcamp, we also offer them theblackcommercenetwork.com where people can sign up and actually sell products from black-owned businesses on their Facebook page and get a commission. There are people who make a living by taking stuff that other people make, other black people make, and selling it on their social media.

We have blackcrowdfunders.com where you can actually raise money through a crowd funding campaign at blackcrowdfunders.com. These are all ways that we set the tone for future generations.

Instead of being consumers of content, we must create it. For example, I can use Instagram to disseminate information and create content. I have 50,000 followers on Instagram. I use Twitter sometimes because my Facebook posts automatically tweet. I also use Periscope. I also have over 1,300 free videos with quite a bit of useful information.

My point is that there are numerous ways, most of them are free, that you can share information with young people. But, we must get back to being a culture that reads and analyzes. This too is not overly complicated.

In some of my Periscope discussions, I will literally grab Dr. Anderson's book *PowerNomics* or *Black Labor, White Wealth*, and I will read a little paragraph, and I'll talk about the paragraph. You see what I mean? I'll talk about what I just read, so we have discussion-like groups sometimes. I do that with my students a lot and you can do it with your children. Sometimes if you can't get a person's attention one way, you have to find alternative ways to get their attention.

But whatever you do, don't assume that it won't take hard work and consistency. Make sure that you are willing to put skin in the game. I'm going to tell you, to build a network, it does take investment. A lot of people want to build empires, but they don't want to put no money into it. That's a hard way to build anything. I swear, I never thought I would make as much money as I've made and be as broke as I was for a very long time.

I used to get paid at Syracuse University, and I made good money at Syracuse, like over $100,000. I put all of my money into my business, every penny. I wasn't waiting on someone else to invest in me. I just knew that that was not a winning strategy based on what I had seen. I wasn't waiting for a grant, sponsorship, a sugar momma, or a venture capitalist to come along. I was like, "Uh-uh, I got to move forward. I got to go."

My mentality always was, "Look, if you can't get a plane ticket, you can always ride a bike. You can always get on your bike and just go hard. Pedal your ass off," and that was my thing. I just said, "Okay, if you can build a CNN on a multi-billion-dollar economic foundation, then you can also build a baby CNN with a $5,000 foundation. Just instead of reaching 10 million people or whatever, you're reaching 10,000." Take one step at a time.

What I'm trying to say to you is you have to start where you're at. I see a lot of people that tell me that they have these great dreams and visions that they want to build and create, and I applaud that. I want you to dream big. Always have a dream. I want you to have the audacity to have a dream. Just practice that. Just start right there.

For some people, the only dream they have is waking up and surviving through the day or paying the utility bill on Friday. That is not a dream. That's not a way to live. Don't do that. Find a dream that's impossible. Find something. Pick a dream that's slightly unreachable, one in which you feel like, "Man, I can't really do this, but I'm just going to go on faith." That's where faith is valuable.

A lot of people say that faith is a bad thing because it's associated with some of the foolery that we see in some churches, but faith is a great thing. Faith is what got me through. We must instill the power of faith in our youth. Many of them walk around purposeless. Of course money is not everything, but if we can provide our young people with ways to achieve their own freedom and autonomy then we can give them hope even in the dimmest and bleakest of circumstances.

I remember growing up in Louisville, Kentucky which is also Muhammad Ali's hometown. The spirit of Ali carries me right now. They say it's that fighting spirit that drives me. Let me explain.

When I was little I used to watch his movie. Have you seen "The Greatest" where he played himself? I remember they had that song, "I believe the children are our future. Teach them well and let them lead the way..."

I remember watching that when I was little, and I remember seeing Ali. I was so proud because he was from my hometown, and I remember seeing this man who came from my city, my little town and literally shook the world. I mean, he literally had people all over the globe who admired him who didn't even know him. Yet, they thought that what he was doing was absolutely powerful and amazing.

He had such an impact, and that inspired me. That plays a big part in who I am now. In his film, he said, "I'm doing this for the children on the next generation," and I thought about it, and I said, "Wait a minute. I'm one of those kids. I'm one of those children from the next generation, and he's inspiring me, so that works. That definitely works!"

Now I'm inspiring the children for the next generation, so if you got your little eight-year-old that's watched a podcast, or they're taking the class from me or whatever, then that's who we're doing this for because I want to be old and gray, and sitting on the dais at some event where they're giving me some sort of lifetime achievement award, and all these young people are coming up and saying, "I grew up on Dr. Boyce. I grew up on x, y, z," or, "I remember the first time I mama introduced me to x, y, z."

It's not so much about me, though. I don't want to make it about me. It's really about all of us just realizing that we can do this. We cannot just win. I don't like words like "equality." I'm not in the struggle for equality. I could care less about equality. We are not talking about black people having equality. I don't want equality.

Actually I don't want to get equal in the game. I don't want to tie the score. I want to win. I want to go beyond equality. I want to actually have a team that is so tight and our execution is so precise that we are off the charts in terms of our preparation and capability. As such, we literally are blowing the other teams out by 20 points. I do believe we have the blueprint.

That's the key. That's what I want you to understand. I thought about these things, and we've all thought about these things, right? But I thought about them and I realized that we have everything we need. We have everything we need.

You have to have the attitude that says, "No, we're not sitting around feeling sorry for ourselves. We're not sitting around getting upset, and being bitter or resentful because somebody said something about us." Who cares what they think about you? This is competition. Your competitor is never going to like you. The more you start winning, the less they're going to like you.

The more you start pulling ahead and scoring points, the more they're going to cheat. The more they see you hoisting up the trophies, the more they're going to talk bad about you and try to undermine you, try to get you thrown off your game, try to distract you. Do you understand that?

A lot of people are able to manipulate the fact that black people are so sensitive. We're very sensitive. We're really can be a hypersensitive community in the sense that if somebody says one thing about black people, we get all mad. We're up in arms, and blah, blah, blah.

I understand. I'll get mad if you say something about me if you pay my bills. That's the rule. If you pay my bills, and you don't like me, and you talk shit about me, then I'm going to have a problem with that because you pay my bills, and that infuriates me that somebody who pays my bills is talking bad about me. Conversely, if you don't pay my bills, I don't really care. I just don't care.

Someone once asked me, "Why did you get fired from Syracuse University?" I don't know if you would call it fired, but I did raise hell. At universities, they have this thing called tenure. You get tenure after you've been there for seven years if they decide to give you that promotion. When I came into Syracuse, they had a huge problem with racism in the Business School, which they still do. It's still pretty racist.

They had seven departments in the Business School. Not one of these departments had ever given tenure to a black man in the entire history of that department, so you had a real problem with black exclusion. Somebody in the university had a shift in consciousness, and they said, "Wait a minute. We don't have any Negroes around here. We don't have any black people. You don't have a single black person on the entire faculty in any department in the Business School. That's weird. Why are you excluding black people?"

What they did was they gave them money, and they mandated that they go and they hire a black person, so they hired three. Three of us came at the same time. We were like the Little Rock Nine walking up in the Business School because we didn't have any other black people around to mentor us, no one to explain the ropes, no one to tell us about the culture, no one to mentor me— none of that. I would see white guys that would get promoted because they would just get in. Somebody would take them under their wing and mentor them and protect them. We didn't have any of that.

I went in there ready to conquer the world—I was ready to roll. I already knew that I was good at what I did, maybe a little bit cocky. I am not going to lie. I was 31. I was a 31-year-old hot shot Ph.D., top of my class. I was smarter than my professors when I was in graduate school. I'm not making that up.

I found myself having to teach the people who were supposed to be teaching me. I recall saying, "No, actually the way the theory is broken down is like this." They weren't t ready for that. They weren't ready for the Black young man to be the smartest one in the room. They're just not. That does not sit well with some people, and I'm not bragging. It's just the honest to God truth.

I got in trouble when I was in graduate school because I was so smart—paradoxical, but true. There was this famous professor from Stanford who came through, and he did his research presentation, and he was wrong. He did a study, or he did a test, a statistical test that was wrong. He did it wrong. I just sat there quietly. I didn't say anything because students aren't really supposed to talk in these little sessions, not to mention that I was the only black person in the room.

The he conducted was related to race. It talked about black people, and I was like, "Man, do I want to say something." I know if I open my mouth, they're going to get mad at me, and I don't want to disrespect this guy, so maybe if I say it politely, it will be okay.

It wasn't okay. I told him professionally and he froze. I remember the look in his eyes was like, "Okay, who is this guy, and why is he talking?" I said, "Well actually, your study, if you did the methodology like this, it would probably be better because the way you did it was wrong," and I explained to him why it was wrong.

I used an analogy to help him understand why it was wrong. It was a funny analogy, but I wasn't laughing at the dude. I didn't laugh at all, but I said it, and I explained it, and it was a perfect explanation, and everybody in the room laughed except two people, me and him. I did not laugh. We both knew I was right.

This guy goes to lunch with a bunch of people in the department, and he's like, "Who is that guy?" because he was embarrassed. He felt like they were laughing at him. I wasn't laughing at this dude. I'm not going to laugh at nobody. I was respectful, but oh my God, it was so funny.

So my evaluations, which used to be stellar and used to read, "Boyce is the best. Boyce is the smartest. Boyce is the most capable" morphed into "Boyce is okay, but he needs to learn how to keep his mouth shut" or "Boyce is a troublemaker." Yeah, it was bad.

Being younger and more radical, I did not fully grasp the politics of academia. Believe it or not, I was even more radical then than I am now. The difference is that I can just articulate my ideas a little bit better now. I was being radical then, but I wasn't wrong. I was respectful and I was right. I was correct, so why was I being punished because I said something that was right?

My chair actually got it. I can remember my chairman was one of those "good white folks," so to speak. He really wasn't taking sides. He was hearing me out, and I was like, "I don't understand this. This doesn't make any sense. Where was I wrong? Explain to me what I said was wrong." They couldn't do that. I even emailed a Nobel Prize winning economist at the University of Chicago who was an expert on that issue.

I said, "Look, this is what I said. This is what methodology I said he should use. This is why I said it was wrong. Was I incorrect?" He said, "No. You were right. It's common sense. Anybody who knows this methodology should know this."

That's when I really learned a lesson about racism and its connection to economic freedom. It wasn't about right and wrong. You think you live in a country that is built on justice. It was not built on justice. America is not built on fairness and equity. America is built on power. Power gives you the ability to decide what's going to be fair; what's going to be unfair; what's going to be right, and what's going to be wrong.

War is not about who's right; it is about who's left, meaning who can decimate who and then rewrite the book on what is right, what is fair, and what is accurate. That is why what I learned.

I went through hell on this. I almost didn't get my Ph.D. because of that. It was all political. They were trying to push me out of the program. The only thing that saved me, and I love this man to this day, was my relationship with W.C. Benton. W.C. Benton is at The Ohio State University. To tell you how deep the racism was, he was the only black professor, at that time, to be tenured in the history of The Ohio State University Business School.

That's how racist these places are. They'll give the promotion to hundreds of white people, but they only pick one black person and think that there's nothing wrong with that. There is a lot that is wrong with people who think that this is acceptable.

No, you're mentally ill. You're blocking out black people, and you're running around lying and saying that black people aren't qualified when you are really messed up in the head to think that no black person on the planet is capable of doing this job. Something is wrong with you! It's not that something is wrong with us.

Some people want to make it about us as Black people, but it's really about you and the mental illness that you're refusing to address that was passed down to you by your ancestors. Period. W.C. Benton went hard for me. He protected me, and he went in and told them, "You know what? If you keep messing with Boyce then you're going to have a problem," because he had power, and he was a real black man. He was a real man. He stood up.

A lot of Black people get in these positions, and they just want to assimilate and fit in. They sit back and they, "Oh, you know what? What happened to you was really certainly unfair, and I would stand with you, but I just can't because it's going to keep me from getting my job or getting my promotion, and blah, blah, blah." That's what they do.

We will watch each other get lynched in a minute. We will be sitting up in corporate America. The corporate Negroes will be sitting there watching it all go down. We will watch a black person get torn to pieces over BS and won't do a word, or won't say a word, won't do a thing. We won't make any sort of meaningful effort to help that person, but he didn't do that.

This man went and had my back. I love him for it. I will always love him for it. In fact, he also taught me something that I never forgot, which reminded me about the importance of black people, especially men, not feeling sorry for ourselves. He said, "Boyce, when I was in the Marines, we learned that even if you're surrounded, even if you know you're going to die, you fire your gun until every bullet is out of that gun. Even if you know ... You never surrendered. You never just give up. You just keep firing until you run out of bullets."

That's what I kept with me all throughout my life. Even when I felt surrounded, even when I felt like I wasn't going to win, even when I felt like I was going to get obliterated, I keep firing until every bullet comes out of that gun, so you might kill me, but I'm going to take a whole bunch of y'all in the process. And when our children watch us that is what they need to see.

When I was at Syracuse I said, "You know what? I'm a waste. I'm an absolute waste as a black scholar if I don't address the black community. The black community needs me too much for me to walk away from them. I cannot do that. I cannot, in good conscience, do that," so all of my work centered on black people. I wrote some research papers on standard asset pricing models, and financial theory, and the stock market, and all that. That's what I teach in my classes right now, but beyond that, when I was going in public and going on national TV, I was talking about the issues that affected black people.

I had a choice. I could have played along and acted as if race didn't matter or I could have advocated on behalf of those who did not have my same platform or access.

This became painfully clear in 2005. Hurricane Katrina went down. I wanted to talk about Hurricane Katrina. I didn't really care so much about just talking about businesses and mutual funds and act like Katrina didn't happen. I could not pretend that black people did not die in the streets in Katrina.

There were black bodies floating in the water in the streets of Katrina. Why would I not address that if I'm a black scholar and I'm on CNN? Are you out of your damn mind? That created chaos and conflict. That created discomfort for people who were not used to working with an outspoken black person. They were not used to a black professor or a black business scholar talking about social issues like that.

It led to some conflict, some discord, and it really got ugly. You can Google all of it because it became public fodder. I had to tell them, I said, "You don't have a single scholar on this entire campus in the history of this university who is as well-known as me in terms of what I'm contributing to the world, but yet you're still trying to somehow convince me that I'm not qualified for this job."

I said, "Look, I'm not offended by this behavior. I understand. Your racism makes you mentally deficient. It makes you ignorant. It makes you incapable of evaluating what a qualified black person looks like, so I'm not angry at you for that. It's not your fault. Your ancestors gave you that mental illness, that disease, but for the sake of other black people who need these jobs, I encourage you to ask yourself a basic question: Why is it that in 100 years of existence you have not given a promotion to a single black person?"

I added, " Why have you somehow allowed people to come and tell you that every single black person to apply for this job, every single black person to try to get a promotion, every single black person who tried to survive in this particular business school was unqualified for whatever reason? Why would you even believe that? It's your racism and the delusional dimension of that racism that leads you to even think that that is logical."

I broke it down, and I didn't get offended by it. I also said, "I'm not going to be quiet about this. The way you're behaving, the way you're treating me, I think you think I'm going to be quiet," because in our industry they don't want black people to become too outspoken. They blackball you, so many black scholars are afraid to speak up because they're scared of being blackballed. They don't want other universities to not want to give them jobs because they can't imagine a life outside of academia.

Black people were not raised to develop institutions. I had been studying entrepreneurship as a way to protect myself because I knew the shit was going to hit the fan. I knew it was going to go down. I knew that I wouldn't be allowed to be around that long because the institutions weren't really ready for people who do what I do.

I could be a little boy and run out here and pick a fight and then get mad because they hit me back, but instead, as a man I felt like, "Shoot, if I was them and I thought the way they think, I probably would wouldn't want me around either. I probably would be offended by me as well because the way they are trained to see the world, they're not able to see what I see, and they don't have an obligation to even try to see what I see."

To be honest, the belief that academicians are all open-minded, thoughtful, and scholarly doesn't always apply, especially in those bureaucratic spaces. I knew that I had to protect myself. I thought, "I'm not going to lose my sanity over this. You're not going to have me running around feeling pissed off and ready to punch holes in walls and all that. You don't have that power over me. I'm controlling this. I'm the dominant party right now. I'm the one who's going to have you in your office. You might be in your office mad as hell because of something I did because I'm not playing ball within the game that you set up for me. I'm not going to go in here and wine and cry about, 'Oh, diversity and discrimination.'" Yeah, it was discrimination. Yeah, it was real, but I saw it as war.

I saw it as me walking into someone else's house and trying to move the furniture around. I know that no sane man is going to let you walk up in his house and move the furniture around, so I created options for myself, and I fought them like hell. I went public with it, not for myself because it wasn't about me. I didn't want to make it about me. Even when reporters would call me I talked to them openly and honestly. I believe the truth will set you free.

I really believe in doing your best to just tell the truth about everything, so I would just tell them the whole story, and then they'd say, "Dr. Boyce, 'so-and-so' in the administration is trying to say that the reason you didn't get tenure is because you didn't publish in enough journals, and you didn't do this and didn't do that."

I said, "Look, let's not make it about me. Let's pretend like I haven't been working my ass off for the last x number of years dedicating my life to this profession, that I'm not getting support from the best leading scholars on the planet. Let's pretend like I'm unqualified. Fine, but what I want you to do is this. I want you to go look at the hiring record of that business school. I want you to go back 100 years and calculate how many African Americans, not foreigners, not minorities, not Africans. How many African-American people have they ever given a promotion to?"

I said, "Based on my assessment, you're going to find either zero or one, maybe one." They said that there might have been one like in 1965 or some crazy shit, but I don't believe it. I had never seen this guy, but either way the fact of the matter is that the fact that the number is so low tells you that that's an institutional problem. That's their problem. It wasn't my problem.

As I think back over this period in my life and how it connects to *Black American Money 2*, I think about the good that came out of the situation. Basically what was beautiful about it was the fact that after I went through my first fight, the chancellor got nervous. We talked. We worked it all out in a certain way. After my fight was done, the very next year they hired more black administrators than I think they've ever hired in the history of that school, more black administrators, new faculty and everything.

A whole lot of black people got opportunities at Syracuse because I took that fight on. That made me proud. I was really happy about that because I know that not every black person has the stomach to fight the way I was fighting with them.

I was a single man, so I was like, "I don't care if I'm living in a cardboard box eating ramen noodles every day. I'm going to be all right. I been poor before. I am not scared to be poor. I been homeless before. At least I got a place to live."

A lot of us are never trained to have our own business. We're never trained to know how to build something of our own. We're trained to get all this education that's within the context of a white supremacist system. Then you end up with that degree, that advanced degree, and you think you're strong, but you're actually quite vulnerable because if they take those opportunities away from you because you're outspoken or because you just don't fit in, then what are you going to do? You don't even know how to start a business.

My feeling is, just keeping it 100%, if you're black in this country and you don't know how to start a business, then you're asking to be victimized. You're begging to be exploited and mistreated. What I would just say to every black person, I don't care if you got a GED or a Ph.D., go take a class on how to start a business. Just learn the very basics. Focus on building something of your own. Get together with your friends the same way you have the courage and the confidence to go start law school and medical school, or to go get your bachelor's, MBA, whatever degree you have, you can also have the courage to sit down and learn how to start a business.

My family and I get together every week, and we have family business meetings. We look at ourselves like we're like the people on *Dallas,* specifically J. R. Ewing's family. In our minds, even if we don't have two nickels to rub together, we have an empire, and we had this before the name "Boyce Watkins" meant a thing.

Before the spotlight, the name-recognition and the influence, we were already thinking in that way and growing in that direction. Believe in your own greatness. You're special. Stop thinking that having a job makes you special or that it makes you better. That has nothing to do with your greatness. You haven't even tapped into your potential as a black person. You're meant to be a king. You're meant to be a queen. You're not meant to be average. Understand that and understand that our children are watching.

CHAPTER 6

THE IMPORTANCE OF ECONOMIC PARTERSHIPS

Having a good paying job seems to be the crux of the American Dream for most people. Getting paid every two weeks and having good benefits is the golden ticket. Unfortunately, we have bought into this narrative so much that we will stay at jobs that we hate, work with people who do not respect us, and report to supervisors who are incompetent. That sounds more like a nightmare than a dream.

Yet, many of us do not seriously consider working for ourselves. We work for others instinctually because that's been built into our cultural DNA over the last 400 hundred years. We're very good at working for other people. That's why everybody wants us to work for them.

Fear of failure is a driving force. Most people I know are just scared to fail. Few people are doing what they actually started off and intended to do in the beginning of their lives because of the fear of failure. I'm not sitting here trying to say that fear of success is not a thing. I'm just here to say that if you set out to do something why wouldn't you want to be successful? I mean success doesn't hurt, it's not that bad. Why are you scared of it? It doesn't make any sense to me.

It's like setting out to learn a new hobby. The idea is to master it, not to fail at it. But if you don't try, you will never know.

Most black business fail because they do not have the capital that is needed for long-term sustainability. You must raise the capital that you need to do what you got to do. I would say that this becomes the biggest challenge. I know that with our business, we didn't always have the capital that we wanted to have to do what we were trying to do, and that would cause frustration at times because there were expansion opportunities that we had where I would say "My God if we had an extra million dollars right now there's so many ways we could make more money."

But sometimes you have to wait. But actually building a business without external investors, that's what they might call boot strapping the business. And boot strapping takes longer, but it's actually a better way to raise a business sometimes because you're not indebted to other people.

Because I would say that the number one problem for black businesses is the lack of access to capital, you have to be very creative about how you raise your capital or how you raise your money. I know that when I started my business my job was my first source of capital. I cut down my bills; I cut down unnecessary spending. I put that money toward my business. In fact, I couldn't even really enjoy my earnings.

It's so funny. I almost got married but I couldn't really get married because I was like *man I don't have enough money because my financial mistress is taking all the cash and I don't really know if I could be married and have a person next to me who's worried about every penny I put into the business*. Because I took a lot of risks in order to be successful did not mean that someone else would be willing to do the same.

It's very hard to become successful at a certain level without taking some chances. You shouldn't take dumb risks, you should take what they call calculated risks. But a calculated risk is still a risk and not everybody's built for that. In the black community, we don't have a lot of people who think entrepreneurially.

Your family is your first small business. You've got to manage that business in terms of who you allow yourself to link up with. In terms of the critical partnerships, whether it's family members or other people, make sure you link up with people who have a value system similar to yours. That means that if you have a business or if you are thinking about a business partner, you should be equally yoked. You know we're good at that already when it comes to religious values?

I'll see people who will say "I will not get married to somebody who is not equally yoked ." Meaning that if you don't go to church then we can't be together. I think that's fine; I mean it is what it is. I'm not judging that, but I also think you might want to be equally yoked in terms of your goals in life. If one person is a risk taker and the other person is scared of his own shadow then that's going to cause problems—that's going to cause a divorce.

Most of my friends in their 40s, who got married when we were in our 20s, are divorced right now. It is probably close to 80% and half of the other 20 percent have dead marriages, so you've got to be extremely careful, especially if you're young. Be careful about the partnerships you chose.

These partnerships extend beyond just romantic relationships and family. You will also enter into business relationships and contractual agreements with financial institutions like banks.

No matter what you do, I would say be careful who you build with. Try to imagine the best manifestation of your vision and what it will cost—in terms of time, money and energy—to make it come to fruition.

Because you can always grow beyond that. You can always add and develop beyond what you have already started with. When I start anything I don't try to build an empire in the first weekend. You know what I do is I say, "Okay let me build a tiny little thing."

If I could make this tiny little thing profitable then there's a natural multiplier there. There's a natural flip. Warren Buffet, became the richest man in the world because of this practice. Tiny Flips is how he makes more money in three days than Lebron James makes in a year. Warren Buffet did not start off doing ten billion dollar deals; he started off doing ten dollar deals. I'm not kidding. Look up his biography. After, the ten dollar deal worked out, he grew that into a hundred dollar deal. Then he started doing 300 dollar deals, thousand dollar deals, and beyond.

Some people rely on others via crowd funding—this too is a type of economic partnership. I would say you may want to look for partners in this process. I think that gofundme or crowd funding can help (blackcrowdfunders.com). I think people, including strangers, can get excited about your vision. You may want to pay a little bit of money, maybe a couple hundred bucks maximum, to have somebody help you make a really creative, exciting video. That will help people see the vision behind what you're doing so maybe you can get people to make some donations that will help this thing go up.

The African American museum that they built in D.C. is an example of why economic partnerships can generate tangible results over a short period of time. They raised money for the museum and even though it is partially publically funded, many private individuals and corporations donated heavily to its creation

A lot of people gave money from Oprah Winfrey to Fox News. Now y'all know I had an issue with that right? I was actually at the opening and, yes, I was being a little bit of a hater—at least I felt like I was anyway. I was like "Wow, Fox News gave 10 million dollars for this. What exactly do you get with a building that's built with money from Fox News?"

I'm not sure, but my point is that this is an example of a prototype of how something can be developed through partnership donations.

Now when you start to build a business, be sure to factor in your costs for supplies, a building, and personnel. I think you also want to think about your plan B, C, D and E on revenue generation. Again, be creative and sit down with other people. In fact, I'm telling you to make the time to have meetings with your family. Please, sit down and have a family business meeting.

Being a family unit isn't just about hanging out. At the family meetings that we have, we'll get together; we'll get some pizza, watch a movie, and hangout. We have fun but then we talk about our businesses and we brainstorm because good ideas get laid on the table and everybody walks away feeling refreshed and encouraged.

Perhaps you don't belong to a close family; the good news is that there are other ways to apply this so that everybody still walks away feeling inspired with new ideas and new partnerships. Networking events are times for you to share with friends and trusted colleagues. Think of your time together as opportunities for you to build empires. I would say get together with some other people and brainstorm on all of the different ways you can make money from your business concept.

For example, there is a lady named Eunique Jones. She has a platform called *Because of Them, We Can*. She has these images of historical black figures and little children dressed in clothes that match the historical figure. And then she puts out memes that go viral on Facebook and she's able to sell all kinds of apparel from backpacks to T-shirts to everything else. Her social media network becomes a tertiary partner in promoting her products.

For a person who may want to take a concept and make it a reality, I say go for it, even if it is something as far reaching as starting a museum. To me, a museum is something that is inspirational; it's something that's informative. It translates into opportunities to offer courses, books, apparel, events, all kinds of stuff beyond the gift shop. That's just my two cents; you may want to give that some thought.

Far-reaching ideas are often the best because they are creative and original. There is a strong possibility that no one else is doing it because it is so far out of the box.

I actually started one of my most successful ventures thinking beyond the status quo. I had 5 thousand dollars and we put it into developing financialjuneteenth.com. It is a website and the key is knowing how to monetize your skills. *Financial Juneteenth* has probably made us 300 thousand dollars off of that initial 5 thousand investment. That's one example.

Partnerships are not always, exclusively, about money. Many partnerships are born out of two people who have complementary skills. We actually have a course in the black business school called *Great Black Writers*. I partnered with Dr. Tyra Seldon who is a prolific writer, author, and small business owner. She is an English Professor who taught writing for years. As a writer, I also understand the nuances of the industry, especially the branding and marketing side. I asked Dr. Seldon to partner with me to create a course that would benefit people who are interested in generating income writing curriculum, blogging, writing books, and everything else writing related. This partnership is a win-win because we are both using our skills. Think of someone that you might want to partner with to jumpstart your business idea.

I'm not talking about a play to get rich scheme. I'm not good at being money hungry because money doesn't matter that much to me. I am talking about being intentional and purposeful. Money matters to the extent that it creates the ability to shape your environment and provide you with what you need. It allows you the ability to define your life instead of your life being defined by your work. I know of too many people who can't take family vacations because they have to work and don't have enough vacation days. This makes it almost impossible to have a work-life balance.

    I think life needs to be the big brother and work needs to be the little brother. Right? And when life is the big brother and work is the little brother then you can work all of the time, but you're not really working; you're actually living. People think I'm a workaholic, but I'm not a workaholic. I'm actually a lifeaholic. I live.

    I'm just living, on a given day you might think I worked 13 hours that day. But I didn't. Actually I worked three hours then I took a nap and then I worked another hour and a half and then I went and watched a movie on *Netflix* and called one of my friends and then I worked another hour and a half. And then I went and did something else.

    Do you see what I mean?

    Ultimately that's a more natural way to live anyway. This is my mindset when I create new projects. For example, I created the *Your Black World Network* because I wanted to quit my damn job and I needed a way to pay the bills. And I know I can write and I know I know finance. I'm like, I'm going to write about finance. I'm not going to wait for somebody to give me a job writing about finance. I'm going to create a job and I'm going to have a blog and I'm going to figure out how to monetize it. I sent my assistant to some classes with Google.

    We focused on how to put ads on a blog so you can make money off the advertising and basically that's what we did and now it generates revenue every month and it works well. YouTube is great. I know a lady who quit her job because she was really mad at white people. She had this real issue with white men. She would talk about all this stuff on YouTube and I said monetize your YouTube blog.

    The reality is that as long as you work for someone else, you are vulnerable. Because you know you're going to get fired if you keep talking a certain way, especially if you are perceived as being too radical. Those white people are going to fire you. You aren't going to be able to keep no job working for white people talking like that.

Eventually, my friend did quit her job; they pushed her out. Now she makes more money on her YouTube channel than she did on her job.

Now it's a better life work mix because she loves doing this. She did this for free now she's paying her bills with this. That's what you want—that's the value of entrepreneurship. That's why it's mandatory that you make sure your child knows how to start a business before the age of 12. I'm not talking about optional. I'm not talking about something good to do. I'm talking about something you have to do. You have to do this.

Because when you understand how business models are created, it takes away the whole black box mindset on where money comes from. We are trained to think that the rich people keep the process behind a curtain. There's this imaginary black curtain and they hand money out to you.

And you just know the money is coming out the curtain because you're showing up to work every day, but they don't show you the mechanism behind the curtain where the money comes from. Once you learn how to make your own money then it's demystified. Then you're like I don't really think I need to go work for the corporation to pay my bills. I can actually develop a small little corporation that can pay my bills even better than working for the big corporation.

That's where understanding business really comes into play. Learn what's behind the curtain. In fact, there's a company called Black Web Solutions (blackwebsolutions.com) that has this process where they know how to put the ads on your blog and monetize it. Now, at that point, you have another issue which is finding a way to get traffic to your blog.

Do your research and reach out to someone who knows how to get traffic to a blog. I learned how to finally sell books by building up my traffic. Before, I couldn't sell any books and I would write a book nobody was buying it. It was like crickets.

Then I learned certain tactics that allowed me to build my brand consistently and also sell books, enough books to keep the business going.

I don't think of myself as a person who writes a book. Instead, I think of myself as a person who constructs an idea. And an idea can be manifested in a multitude of ways. An idea can manifest as a book. It can manifest as a blog, a film, a chorus, a live event or even a t-shirt design. There's a lot of different ways to manifest a concept.

I think about Walt Disney. When you think about Disney, you don't think about a singular entity or product. The Disney model actually is one that is very appealing to me and quite intriguing. Disney created a brand. Let's think about Mickey Mouse in particular.

I like Mickey Mouse actually because it was an idea that Mr. Disney came up with after he, literally, had just been fired from his job. He hit his low point on the corporate plantation not just because he was fired, but because someone could easily steal his intellectual property. It was not uncommon for people to take your ideas. In fact, it was legal because everything you did belonged to the company you worked for—this is still true today.

Disney took this long train ride all the way from L.A. to New York for this big meeting. He thought that he was going to get a raise and a promotion; instead, he was let go. Can you imagine the emotions he felt when he showed up thinking that he's going to get rewarded and instead, they whacked him. Painful, right?

He went in there; they fired him and they took all of his intellectual property. He's at his ultimate low point. Well, as he was heading back on this train to L.A., he said to his mother, "You know ma, I think I want to create this character. It's going to be a mouse and I think I'm going to call him Mortimer Mouse." And his mother was like "Mortimer Mouse? That's too long just call him Mickey."

And that is how Mickey Mouse was born. I bet if you look up the market value of Mickey Mouse, it's probably worth about 5 or 6 billion dollars. At a moment when he could have given up and just quit, he actually created one of the world's most iconic and recognizable brands.

This man's idea began on a train where he just decided to create a character that's a mouse. Now, you can buy Mickey Mouse dolls, Mickey Mouse tablecloths, Mickey Mouse T-shirts, and you can go see movies with Mickey Mouse in them. Let's not forget that you can go to theme parks and see Mickey Mouse. Mickey Mouse T.V. shows morphed into the very popular and lucrative Disney cable channel.

One idea with numerous manifestations is also an option for you. I would encourage you to think in the multimedia framework. Don't think of yourself as just as a writer or just as a T.V. show host or just as a blogger or just as a radio host.

Of course, you can do all of those things. I'll use myself as an example. Our YouTube channel makes a lot of money. You know we get three million views a month on our YouTube channel. I think people watched over 15 million minutes of video on our channel this month. We have our blogs. We probably hit 150 million views of our different blogs. I also have a podcast on Sound Cloud. I do stuff on Facebook Live and I distribute vital information via text message.

What I'm saying to you is that whatever your ideas are, I would spend time really being a student of business so you can find a lot of different angles to use. Find numerous and varied ways to develop yourself and that includes investing in yourself and finding good partnerships. This way, you don't have to be a spectator. You, too, can find a way to do what everybody else is trying to do.

Most people are trying to feed their family and avoid having to go be a slave to the white man. My job is to give you tips and tools that will help you do that.

Let's look at the Native American community; they have been hammered unfairly by this government and by this society. I think that there has to be some spiritual healing there.

They lost the greatness of their ancestors because it was systematically stamped out of them. It wasn't their decision to do this. Alcoholism, drug addiction, and poor communal choices eventually took their toll. They have a lot in common with black people. They're going through a lot of what we go through, but it seems to be more demoralizing and annihilating in some communities than others, taking on physical, emotional and spiritual manifestations.

How do you reignite the hope? If you have no hope then you're going to give up. If I don't believe things could ever get better why would I even try? Right?

You reignite the hope and then you start to lay the skill. Actually I start with hope and then I go into love. I show you I love you. I show you how to love yourself then we go into building. Building together, which also requires courage; it requires vision and it requires ways to remain motivated. I actually have probably more in common with a preacher than I do with a finance professor. At the end of the day, I am concerned about how are we going to inspire one another to be strong and to build what we need in our homes and our communities?

I don't know what happens when you die or if you go to heaven. Are the streets paved with gold? Do you get 72 virgins? Can you kick it with Tupac or Martin Luther King, Jr. while drinking mimosas on the beach? I don't know what happens in heaven; I have never been there. I've read what people have said in books and I recall what my pastor told me, but my pastor hasn't been either. I really don't know, but what I do know is that we must do a better job in the here and now,

I do know that after you're done, after you die, the people you love are still going to be here. They're still going to be affected by the choices you make in this life right now. Whether you leave them wealth or don't leave them wealth will affect their economic opportunities and it will determine if they have to start from scratch or not.

Whether you teach them or you don't teach them is going to affect how they see the world and influence their worldviews. Whether or not they feel trapped or they feel free depends on what we do as a people. And so what I would say is that the best way we create a legacy is to live this life in a way where we plant seeds that will harvest in the afterlife in such a way that we will win through the people that we love. We are the ancestors. We just happen to be alive right now.

There are life experiences that we all can learn from. Even I have to stay focused and motivated because when you operate at a certain level and you're trying to be a leader, a king, a queen or an innovator or a game changer, you're going to run into resistance. There's no great man or woman in history who didn't face a tremendous amount of resistance, so the spiritual battle is every bit as important as the intellectual battle.

Because of this engaging in entrepreneurship while having a 9 to 5 is difficult. I highly recommend getting into the culture of business ownership and business development. Think of entrepreneurship like hip hop. Ask somebody what is hip hop?

They can't really tell you; they can just show you. If you say, "How did you become so involved in hip hop?" They might just say, "I don't know. I just grew up around it and I loved the music; I listened to it every day. I lived in the South Bronx and I would see the graffiti, the styles, and I felt the energy."

Hip hop is everything from how you walk to how you communicate to what clothes you wear to what music you listen to. Music is only a small part of hip hop culture right? Just like you have prison culture or you have corporate culture or you have church culture. Church culture is about church hats, the pastor, a choir, and fellowshipping.

Well, the reason you're integrated into those cultures is because your subconscious has been consistently inundated with imagery and stimuli from that culture; it has shaped who you are as a person. It's subconscious.

Entrepreneurship culture is the same way. If you are a 9 to 5 person and you're trying to flip to become an entrepreneur, you need to understand it's going to be an uncomfortable psychological surgery.

You're going to go through a metamorphosis that's going to feel really awkward at first. It is no different from me going out and learning how to be a gangster rapper. It's going to be hard for me to learn how to act like a thug—I am not saying that I will actually do this, but it drives home the point.

Whatever it is I'm trying to be, I have to work to become it. I encourage you to start working slowly, but surely at becoming an entrepreneur. Start studying the craft—it makes sense to start listening to podcasts by entrepreneurs. Every day start reading articles by entrepreneurs, try having conversations with entrepreneurs, find an entrepreneurship group, and start going to meetings on a regular basis.

Inspiration and intellect work together are not separate things. Over time, you'll get better and you'll learn to identify opportunities. You'll even start to see monetary opportunities. You'll also start to see how to build and grow. Entrepreneurship is good because that's one of the quickest ways I've seen to build and make a lot of money really fast.

Student loan debt is a pain in the rear because universities overcharge people now. Universities are robbing the American people and that's just a fact. They're defrauding the American people, in my opinion, because it shouldn't cost you no hundred thousand dollars to go get a four year degree, that's insane.

To jumpstart your business, stop acquiring debt. I wouldn't go back and get an M.B.A. and all this other stuff, no. Entrepreneurship is the new M.B.A. I would rather spend the same amount of time I spent learning in a business school finding other places and avenues to grow in both practical and professional ways.

Learn everything you need to know to do what you have to do. Then when you start a business, you'll have different streams of income and can make a decent amount of money very quickly. This will allow you to chop down that debt fast. It's much easier to become a crackpot entrepreneur than it is to become a professional athlete.

The beauty of it is that if you get good at it, you can do things that you never imagined, like make 100,000 dollars in a month. I never thought that was possible, even as a professor. I didn't do that when I had a job. I've done that as an entrepreneur. It's great, if you're debt is 100,000 dollars then you could knock off all of your debt like that.

And entrepreneurship is fun. It's so much fun. You are missing out if you're not out here really doing new stuff. Try new stuff don't do the same stuff. Don't act like somebody from 1965. You've got to do your own thing.

And one thing you don't want to do is ignore the community that supports you. There is a strongly held idea that the Black consumer is more difficult than his/her peers.

We have to change that mindset. Yes, some people are just difficult and yes, some black people are difficult, but not all black people are difficult. Some black people are, just honestly, confused. Some people are just trained to be straight up coons; they have no love for black people. They are hateful and they're nasty, but we still have to forgive them for they know not what they do.

They, literally, have been trained to think that way; they've been developed into these people. I try my best to love everybody even if they come at me crazy. But it's hard sometimes because we are all human. Sometimes I use tough love and some of you all have seen me do that, but I love us nonetheless and I encourage you not to give up on our community.

I would say you can't give up. It is like loving someone who has been abused who has no dealt with the trauma.

If you love that person then you'll find a way to love through the walls so you can get to the core because I believe at the core, all people want to be good. Spend time also around your people. Find other people that are doing what you're doing. If there aren't people in your industry introduce people to it.

I have had to introduce hundreds of thousands of black people to the value of economic knowledge and financial literacy. When I first started talking about this in 2005/2006, a lot of people were not hearing what I was saying. They were not listening. They were not ready.

I had to show them things that allowed them to say hey maybe this is something I want to learn about. Right? And so a lot of people are students of mine now. Because I was the person that introduced them to another way of looking at the world. And that was partly by design. Not just because I wanted to help people. I love helping people.

Human nature is that people tend to dance with whoever brought them to the party. When I first started, a lot of people were saying that black people were not really going to be interested in financial literacy. They assumed that we only wanted *WorldStar Hip Hop*.

As such, they wanted a gossip site; they wanted all of this other stuff. I said if I introduce them to something better then people will gravitate towards it and that's what I did. I said I'm going to just go in here and grow an audience because I didn't have an audience when I first got started.

Like everyone else, I started with a blank canvas. I had decide what I wanted to paint, the colors I wanted to use, and who I wanted to invite to the table with me. I did not create a masterpiece on my first try, so I had to keep painting, even if it meant grabbing a new canvas and starting over sometimes.

Where ever you are in your journey, do not get discouraged and do not feel like you have to do this alone.

CHAPTER 7

ARE WE REALLY A BROKE PEOPLE?

No one wants to be broken. In fact, we often reject broken things and see them as less desirable, worth less, and not worth our time. So, for the life of me, I will never understand why some black people subscribe to and even embrace the idea that black people, are perpetually, a broke people?

What group of people actively and consistently embrace their own degradation? We need to talk about this.

I tend to believe that there are times when we have to talk shop. I believe there are times when black people have to get together and have conversations about things that affect all of us.

I saw that there was a popular discussion about black wealth. The article was in *The Nation* and it had been read and shared thousands of times. Some of you probably read the article; it was both thought-provoking and troubling.

The article, in a nutshell, claimed that the average black household would need 228 years to accumulate as much wealth as white people have right now. Let me repeat that: it would literally take you 228 years to get to the same place where your white peers are right now.

It's not saying that in 228 years, you will be equal to white people. It's saying that at our current growth rates, it will take 228 years to get what they have right now. It's very different from saying that you're going to be equal in 228 years. I hope you understand the difference there.

Imagine if you are in a race and you're running against somebody that's half a mile in front of you or way out in front of you and somebody says, it's going to take you 228 years to just get to where they are right now. That means that in 228 years, they're going to still be way out in front of you. You're not going to actually catch up.

Ultimately I think that's the first thing that just jumps out at me about this statistic. I assume that they wrote it the way it was intended and it actually makes more sense because when I've studied the wealth gap, and I've been studying this a lot because in the black business school we're actually going to offer a class on building family empires, I am determined to help us get ahead.

There are formulas; there are things you can do. I've studied wealthy people. I've studied self-made wealthy people. Not people who had their daddy leave them a $1,000,000. No. I'm not talking about people like that. I'm talking about people who started with nothing and ended with a lot. People who will start with almost zero or maybe they start in debt and they end up with wealth. That is doable. I think as we have this conversation about the wealth gap, it's very important that we take a second to realize that these problems are not insurmountable.

One of the things that I want to get away from is a trapped mentality. You know they're talking about brothers being locked up in the trap. I think a lot of us are in the trap too. We're in the trap in the sense that we get trapped into believing that where we start off is where we're destined to finish the race.

We're trapped into believing that the only solution to very serious problems is government intervention. Remember that's very different from saying we don't deserve government intervention; we know that we do. We know we deserve reparations, that's a lost conversation. If you hear the debate whether or not we deserve reparations, I'm not going to have that debate with you because to me that's a silly debate.

You steal somebody's stuff; you're supposed to give it back.

Whether we deserve reparations, to me, has nothing to do with the fact that we probably won't get it any time soon. Whether we deserve government intervention should be disconnected from the fact that I don't believe we're going to get government intervention in a meaningful way.

I don't believe that the government is ever going to step up. I don't think these white guys up in congress, Capitol Hill, are going to start solving your problems before they solve their own problems. Believe me, the government is headed to hell in a hand basket. They're making a lot of economic and policy decisions that are going to ultimately destroy this country. They're going to have their own problems to solve and believe me, solving the race problem, is going to remain at the bottom of their priority list or it is going to get kicked off the priority list because they're going to be fighting for their own survival.

I really believe that, because a lot of the decisions they're making are not very intelligent right now. With that being said, the trap mentality again goes back to this idea that we can't fix it; we need the government, the government must do something, policies must change, et cetera. I don't like that mentality. I believe that we can focus on the things about America does provide.

We know America is not a great country. Donald Trump won on a campaign of making America great again. America was never great, but America has never been the worst country in the world to live in either. We have to admit that as well. What does that mean? That means that if you look at America for what it is, if you understand the systems for what they are and how they function, you can position yourself and your family in such a way that you can benefit from the opportunities provided by America.

What does that mean? In the course that I was telling you about on how to turn your child into a millionaire, I realized that instead of just teaching kids about wealth, we must have wealth building programs for children. I realized I need to teach the teachers. I need to teach the parents so that parents can speak to their kids about these issues in a way that's going to put them where they want them to be.

I call it the eight step family wealth building life cycle. One of the most important steps is that before you move forward, before you talk about building wealth, you have to understand the economic system that you're operating in. In a way, I compare it to double dutch jump roping. You ever seen anybody that's about to double dutch? What do they do?

They look and then they hesitate for a minute. They're trying to get in rhythm with the ropes and then they jump in and they're jumping. They're in rhythm because they sat there and they studied the movement of the ropes before they jumped in.

The economic system is the same way. As I was developing the curriculum, I was talking to Dr. Tyra Seldon and she mentioned that quite a few people don't even know what an economic system encompasses. They understand things on a micro-level as it affects their day-to-day lives, but they can't see the bigger picture or the macro-level.

They don't even know that they're in an economic system. I thought about that and I said, wow that's a very good point. In other words, they don't have a firm grasp of what a system is or their role in it. So, how can we change something that we don't understand? How can we jump in between the ropes if we don't know what we are supposed to do once we get in between them?

Not only should your kids be made aware that they're in an economic system, they should be made aware of what position they want to play in the economic system.

Here's the thing about America, if you either don't understand the economic system or you don't know that you're even in an economic system then you cannot compete. It's like going out into a football game and you not only don't know how to play football, you don't even know that you're on the football field. Next thing you know, the ball lands in your hands and you're getting crushed from every direction. That's what's going to happen.

Imagine if you were dropped in the middle of the football field or in the middle of a battle field and you don't even know that there's a war. You think it's a picnic and they're literally firing gunshots at each other across the field. You're going to die. You're going to be taken out. The thing about America that's really interesting to me is that America, being the capitalist society, is like this.

I'm not saying capitalism is good or bad. I think capitalism is powerful. I'm not going to say it's good or bad. I think free enterprise is good. Business ownership is good. Industry is good.

Production is good. All these things are good.

Capitalism can be very bad or capitalism can be okay. It depends on how well it's regulated. It's just like fire. If it's regulated and you manage it properly, it's a wonderful thing. If you don't regulate it and you burn everything up, then you're going to burn the whole house down. Capitalism is analogous to this.

When I saw this article and the number 228 jumping from the headline, I thought about other depressing statistics about how the rich have gotten richer and the poor have gotten poorer and that America's policies tend to favor the rich. I agree with all of that.

My research confirms every ounce of everything that they're saying. The question is, what do you do? What do you do? Okay, we can complain about it and we could talk about it. We should complain about it. We should protest it. Then what?

Every time Hillary Clinton or some Democrat came to your church and wanted to eat barbecue chicken with the pastor and get you to vote for her because you're apparently supposed to because you owe the Democrats your life, did you also bring up this issue of economic disparity?

Seriously, here is what we need to do. Bring it up. Push the issue. Absolutely. Step one: We've complained about it; we've talked about it, but identify one tangible think that has worked. Step two: Think about how you operate and function within our economic system. Are you positioning you and your family to have prosperity and strength as opposed to being victims of hopelessness and devastation?

One of the things that I will never believe is this idea that if you are born poor you're supposed to be poor for the rest of your life.

The reason I disagree with this sentiment is because there's no evidence I've seen that really confirms that. We have systemic factors. We have poor educational systems and we have urban violence. We have different kinds of issues that directly target black people and seek to exterminate us. We know those things exist.

At the same time, there are specific things that people can do that will position their families to be in a better wealth position by the next generation. Here's what's fundamentally true about the economy and the way the economy is structured. If you look at the gap or if you analyze the wealth gap between the rich and the middle class and everybody else, you will discover that the gap is pretty much, consistently, defined by three factors.

The three factors are number one: participation in the stock market. Number two: ownership of real estate. Number three: business ownership and entrepreneurship. It is due to a governmental bias that these factors even play such a prominent role.

You probably will not get rich if you don't invest or if you don't work for yourself. If you work for other people, it's very hard to get wealthy and if you don't invest your money, or opt to just save, that's usually not going to make you rich. Effectively, if you look at those three factors and isolate them, what does that mean?

The stock market, as I point out in a previous chapter, is not something that only rich people are allowed to invest in. There's no whites only sign on the stock market. There's no sign saying that you have to have a $1,000,000 in assets to buy stock. Anybody could buy stock. As a reminder: let's say you went back 30 years, 35, 40 years in time and you said, what if it was 1975 instead of 2017. Let's go back about 40 years ago to 1977. You have a parent or grandparent who just put a $100 a month in the stock market for you. They just invested a $100 a month and didn't worry what stocks they bought. They just bought whatever stock came to mind, just bought random stocks.

Do you understand that after 30 years, according to historical returns in the stock market, you would have about $350,000 in liquid assets that your mother could give to you, your father could give to you? If you go out 40 years, that goes up to about $1,200,000. That's just from stock market participation, that's just $100 a month. Most people can afford a $100 a month. That's $25 a week. Think about how many times you've spent 25 bucks on things that didn't give you anything—that didn't amount to nothing. I've seen people blow $25 or $100, I've seen people spend $25 a week literally eating fast food or going to the club. You go to the club, you're going to drop a 100.

We will spend money very quickly on consumer items. We love to consume. The consuming is not the problem, it's when you consume it you don't invest that you get in trouble. That's when it causes you problems.

The stock market, buying shares, and stock can solve a lot of financial problems, in my opinion, based on historical returns in the market.

Next, there is real estate. Okay, getting involved in real estate is a little tougher because it takes a little bit more capital to do. I can tell you this, Andre Hatchet, who runs the blackrealestateschool.com, teaches a class on how to buy homes and how to buy real estate. Andre Hatchet said that he bought his first home in New York when he was making $15.15 an hour. He set a budget, spent a year and a half saving up money for his house, and then he bought a duplex. It wasn't anything great, but it was property. He was a property owner.

S. Tia Brown, from *Ebony Magazine* who I do *Financial Lovemaking* with, often talks about how she basically went a whole year and said, "I'm going to do my own hair instead of giving my money away to the hair salon." She saved up the money that she would have spent at the hair salon and then went and bought her first property with the savings.

Now she owns several properties in New York. Owning real estate, again, is not something that only rich people can do, but it tends to be something that wealthier people might tend to think about and also, if you really want to learn about making money, you may want to go study self-made millionaires. Again, not the person whose mama or daddy left him money. I'm talking about people who actually started with nothing and ended up with something. Here's a secret about self-made millionaires.

If you took away all of the money that they have and forced them to start the game all over again (the wealth building game), after a decade, they'll have the money again. You understand this?

Simply put, I'm saying that your culture, your habits, and how you see money plays an important part in whether or not you build wealth and how much wealth you build. Again, it does not say that these other factors don't play a role; we know that they certainly do.

What's interesting about this *Nation* story is that they're not really telling you anything new. This is reported every year, not even every year, every two or three months, there's a big story that comes out about how big the wealth gap is. Either that it's not shrinking or it's as big as it was in the 1960s or whatever. That's the funny thing about the wealth gap, the wealth gap is actually growing. It's not even that it's not shrinking fast enough, it's actually growing. It actually grew during the Obama presidency.

What they did in this article is find a creative way to present old information, but it's important information. I'm glad that people are talking about it, but it's not a shocker. Nothing has really changed.

Here's the thing that we have to deal with in our community: You all don't want to be entrepreneurs. We were trained to go out and seek a job, but we were never trained to go create a job. It's not your fault; it's just the world we live in. We got caught up with integration and everything which was our version of 40 acres and a mule. But somewhere along the way, we put aside the value of ownership, not just material possessions, but our collective legacy as a people.

It was nicer to go work for the big corporation and we somehow lived under the false assumption that being close to somebody else's power is the same as actually having power, which isn't true. That job is not yours, that job does not belong to you. You cannot pass that job to your children. That does not belong to your family. That is not an asset for you.

That is not real power; it is borrowed power. Let's be clear about that. It's not your fault that you've been trained to think this way, but understand the consequences of thinking this way. Basically, we are indoctrinated to have an over dependence on an oppressor to pay our bills. This has made all of us economically insecure and it has made many of us economically immature which helps explain the 228 number.

The reason I say economically immature is because, an immature person is somebody who can't take care of themselves. Imagine your 10-year-old running around the house acting like he owns it. Can you see him acting like he's a grown man? You're going to look at him and maybe even say, "You can't even pay your own bills. "

You can't even feed yourself, what makes you think you're a grown man? For black folks, unfortunately we perceive ourselves and others perceive us as a group of people who can't feed ourselves. We can't produce what we need to be able to survive. We can't create jobs because that's just not part of who we are.

I am not saying that we couldn't do it if we put our mind to it. We must put as much energy into learning how to start businesses as we're learning how to dribble basketballs, throw footballs, sing, dance, rap, act and do all of these other things to entertain white people.

If we really put as much energy into being entrepreneurs as we put into being entertainers, we would be the best entrepreneurs on the planet. There is a false assumption that in order to be an entrepreneur, you have an excessive amount of money saved in order to start your business. That's not true. A good entrepreneur is almost like a boy scout or an eagle scout who knows how to start a fire without a match.

Imagine an eagle scout; he's in the woods and he's been trained really well or by somebody in the Navy Seals. He doesn't even need a match to start a fire. The same thing is true with a good entrepreneur. A good entrepreneur can start off with no capital or very little money and start a business and know how to flip it and keep flipping and flipping and flipping until that business becomes something that's substantial.

If you really want to look at this gap and really challenge the gap them you can challenge it politically by talking to your white politicians and the Democrats or other people who keep lying to you every four years. I'm not going to tell you not to, I'm not going to stop you from that. I'm not in those conversations. I'm not going to any of those White House meetings. I'm not going to be invited anyway.

What I will say is that we need to address the culture. We have to realize that there are things you can do as a parent. The other thing too about wealth building that people have to understand is that wealth building is not a game for people who are shortsighted, myopic, or selfish. If all you're thinking about is what you're going to do by yourself in the next five or 10 years, then you're going to see wealth building as the most impossible game you've ever played in your life.

It's like trying to figure out how to run a marathon in 20 minutes. You can't do it; it still isn't going to happen. Wealth building is a game that occurs across generations. If you want to look at families that have empires, remember that these empires were built.

If you study these empires, you will probably notice that they were built over two or three generations. At least one generation was the seminal generation. This person was the workhorse, the grinder, or the one who changed and/or flips the family culture. The one who says, "You know what? I came from this but I'm not of this."

He/she might add, "I'm going to become something better, I'm going to become something stronger so I'm going to work my ass off to build and accumulate something so that I can pass this down to my kids."

Here's the other interesting thing about wealth building and why you need to be careful. 90% of wealthy families lose their wealth with two generations. You tell me what that says about how your mindset plays a part in whether you accumulate wealth or whether you lose wealth?

Why does that happen? Why does that wealth suddenly disappear in a lot of these families? It disappears because the parents or whoever was it that built the wealth had a different mindset from the people who were given the wealth after the first generation was dead.

You work hard; you bust your butt to give your child everything you never had and spoil the hell out of them. Then, you die and they get that big check after you're gone and they blow it all. They spend it all. They consume it all. They're not thinking about accumulating and building. They don't have the same hunger and drive that you might have had and it ultimately causes them to die broke. Ultimately what I want you to really understand is that a lot of accumulation of wealth building really comes down to culture.

Any family that really truly wants to attack this thing and really play this game at the highest levels needs to address the culture of your household. Do you have a culture of investors or do you have a culture of spending and borrowing and consuming? If you have investors and producers and builders and savers in your family, then you're going to accumulate.

If you have spenders and borrowers and consumers, then you're not going to accumulate because you're both in the economic system, it's just that one is the predator and one is the prey. If you want call it that.

Think about it, ask yourself and your family, when my family gets money, what do they do? For example, if they were suddenly given a check for $50,000, what would they think to do with that money? What would they do? Would they say, "Oh wow this is a capital base for our family, we can plant this money in certain places and make it grow over time, because it can grow."

Or would they say, "I can get a new car or oh, let's go to the mall or let's help cousin Pookey buy a new purse. I'm going to help cousin Pookey out."

Think about both of these scenarios and the implications. Think about how we use our money and the things we do with our money.

Culture is everything. Some discuss wealth disparity as a purely political issue, which it is. It really is in the sense that white people stole from us and they owe us. As I have said before, they owe us trillions. They really do. In fact, the probably could not even begin to repay all the money that they've taken from us over time. There's no question about it, I'm in complete agreement with that.

It doesn't have to be an either/or conversation, it can be both/and. Yes, you all owe us and yes, you all did steal our labor, yes I'm going to still stay mad at you all until you all pay us back. While I'm mad at you all and while you're over there not paying us back, we're going to be over here building.

We can control what goes on inside of our own household as it relates to attitudes and discussions about money.

Do you understand? At the end of the day, it's going to be our responsibility to clean our mess up or decide if we want to just sit there and feel bad for ourselves. Personally I really don't want my grandchildren reading this same doom and gloom story about how white people got it all and we don't have anything. I don't want them to grow up in a world like that.

I don't want my children or my grandchildren to feel like white people are just superior to them and that they just have this wonderful life that we can't ever possibly compete with them. I don't want them to feel that way.

It's almost like if you're in a war or if you're in a battle and you know you're surrounded and you know that you might not win the fight, you have a decision to make. Do you just lay down and cry and feel sorry for yourself or do you just fight until you're gone, until the last bullet is out of your gun? I say you tell your children to be empowered and to fight.

You might not have everything you need but when it comes to

fighting this battle, you fill that gun up and you shoot until every bullet falls out the clip. Yes, black entrepreneurs are undercapitalized. Yes, black entrepreneurs have a lot of structural obstacles that keep us from doing the same things that white people can easily do. Is that an excuse for mediocracy?

Black men have every obstacle in front of them that you can imagine, but you are never ever better off not fighting than you are by standing up for yourself and doing the best you can with what you've got. I'm a big believer in that.

Here's the good news. Black people are not that broke. Black people only feel broke when we compare ourselves to what we think white people have.

When you compare what we have to what they have it seems just hopeless. When you look at what black people in America have compared to what the rest of the world has, there's a lot of hope there.

We have that 1.1 trillion in spending power everybody keeps talking about. We've got that. That's a lot of money. If black America were a country by itself, I think it would be like the eighth or ninth richest country in the world. Anybody who says that it's totally hopeless and that we can't do nothing and we're just stuck need to shift his/her perspective. We are builders. What do builders do? They build.

Creating new opportunities for wealth is not difficult. I often tell people to buy their child at least a $100 worth of stock every month form the time that they're born. If you really care, if you really want to do it right, don't make it a $100 a month. I set the bar low because some people feel like black people are so pathetic that we can only meet the lowest expectations.

I don't believe that, but I did set it low so that nobody gets mad at me for setting high expectations for black people or for being elitist. *Oh my God, as if black people can actually rise above the bar. Oh Lord, what am I thinking if I believe in them black people?*

Seriously, I am being realistic because $25 a week is what most people can afford. Buy your child at least a $100 a month worth of stock from the time that they're born and then the other thing that you should do is make sure that your life insurance is paid up. Get at least $100,000, maybe $200,000 or more in life insurance which doesn't cost that much to have.

If you live long enough and you and your child partner on this $100 a month plan in the stock market, according to historical estimates, you will have about $350,000 in the market by time the child is 30. $1,200,000 by the time the child is 40. The child's a cash money millionaire by that point or liquid millionaire. Liquid meaning that they can actually sell these stock and have $1,200,000 in cash. (Yes, I said this in a previous chapter, but I cannot emphasize it enough in *this book*.)

If you pass away or something happens to you, your insurance policy kicks in and then your child gets a quarter of a million dollars or whatever you leave to the child. They're able to take their money and invest it. The key thing is that if you accumulate wealth for your child, make sure you teach your child how to protect that wealth.

If you do not teach your child the things I'm teaching you, then what's going to happen is, you're going to work your ass off and accumulate all this money and leave it to your kids and they're going to blow it. It will be gone.

They're going to making it rain up in the club, doing whatever and spending money on all kinds of nonsense because you never taught them the difference between being a producer and a consumer. You never taught them what investing means. You never taught them about the very simple concept of preservation of capital.

Most institutions in America exist mainly because they have a base of capital that they preserve. Harvard University, over a couple of hundred years, has accumulated a 20 billion dollar endowment. They use the interest off of this money to pay their bills and operating costs. They also have tuition money and grant money coming in.

Ultimately you and your family, if you want to talk about building wealth or having a family empire, need to start now. It's all about building a pile of capital and teaching the heirs to preserve their capital.

For example, my kids aren't really getting access to all of my 'empire' until they're 40-years-old. They'll get access to pieces as time goes on, but studies show that children don't really understand the value of wealth until they're over 40. They're not going to have access to everything until they're past 40. That's where a trust comes into play.

So the next time someone suggests that black people are broke remind them of this: Black people have lots of money and we are determined to spend it. According to the State of the African-American Consumer Report, African American buying power is expected to rise to $1.1 trillion by 2015.

This makes the black community a force to be reckoned with when it comes to the power of earning and consumption. The study was designed to analyze the buying and spending habits of the black community, likely so major corporations can figure out how we think and what we want to buy. The goal at the end of the day, is for corporations to find out how to get your money out of your pocket.

"By sharing, for example, that African Americans over-index in several key areas, including television viewing and mobile phone usage," Susan Whiting, vice chair of information and analytics company Nielsen, told *BlackVoices.com*. "We've provided a better picture of where the African American community can leverage that buying power to help their communities."

The results of the study were released at the 41st Annual Legislative Congressional Black Caucus Foundation Conference.

"Too often, companies don't realize the inherent differences of our community, are not aware of the market size impact and have not optimized efforts to develop messages beyond those that coincide with Black History Month," said NNPA chairman, Cloves Campbell. "It is our hope that by collaborating with Nielsen, we'll be able to tell the African American consumer story in a manner in which businesses will understand, and, that this understanding will propel those in the C-Suite to develop stronger, more inclusive strategies that optimize their market growth in Black communities, which would be a win-win for all of us."

The study concluded that if African-Americans were a country, we'd be 16th in the world in spending power (please refer to Chapter 1 for greater clarity). It also found that African Americans use our cell phones twice as much as whites. As a person who's taught finance at the college level for nearly twenty years, here's what the study's results say to me an why you should care:

1) **African Americans should be sure to harness our vast economic power by targeting our spending to black-owned businesses**. This will help with the black unemployment problem by providing much-needed capital to black companies who can't get financing from traditional sources. White people have proven that they don't like to hire us. A recent experiment by a blogger (Yolanda Spivey) showed that when she changed her profile to appear to be a white woman, the number of job offers she received skyrocketed. This is the struggle we're dealing with, as Washington politicians love to assume that black people just don't want to work.

2) **We should all save and invest our money and not be duped into the "feel-good" domain of mass consumption**. Consumption is like alcohol or a drug: It intoxicates you into an addiction to short-term gratification that leads you to long-term economic slavery. We can't always focus on doing what feels good; we must instead focus on actions that provide a long-term benefit.

3) **We should remember that our financial independence is critical for our spiritual and social independence.** You can never demand your civil rights while simultaneously begging the descendants of your historical oppressors to help you feed your children. Malcolm X told us this long ago, and it's one of the reasons that black America is so blatantly disrespected as a viable political constituency.

In a capitalist society, MONEY-IS-POWER. More importantly, it is the intelligent application of money that becomes critical to the survival and prosperity of our community. If you aren't smart enough to control the power of money, then the power of money will ultimately control you. Don't work hard to become a high-paid slave, for you deserve a better fate than that.

And don't believe the hype that we are inferior to white people. Psychologically, it posits us as victims. We know that we have power. The real question is what do we plan to do with it? How will its use benefit us and others in our community?

It is how we answer these questions that will usher us into the next century. At some point, you have to decide what that future will look like for you. If we all wait around for someone to come save us—like Superman—then I hate to tell you that you will be waiting for a very long time, if not forever. Why?

Because we are powerful people with the intellect, creativity, and genius to build a nation, you cannot tell me that we can't rebuild our families, our communities, and our nation.

It's just that simple.

All of these examples illustrate that there are ways to fix this and tangible ways for us to overcome the wealth gap. There are self-made millionaires in this country and yes, some of them are black. You're not destined to be in poverty. I'm actually glad that *Nation* wrote this article and that it generated conversations in black communities.

I think it's important because if we don't know that a problem exists, how do we solve it? The answer is that we can't and that perpetuates a cycle of helplessness. Great people are not helpless.

I do think that awareness is important, but I also think that there's a point where you have to let go of the politics and just say, what am I going to do for me and family?

CHAPTER 8

MAINSTREAM AMERICA AND THE BLACK DOLLAR

I often think about those things that influence us and that play a vital role in the decisions that we make. I grow tired, in particular, of the ignorant people that we see on TV, the ignorant representations of black people and the fact that mainstream media has brainwashed us into believing that this is our culture.

You may be thinking why is this relevant to *Black American Money 2*? Actually, culture, cultural representation, and who controls the culture has everything to do with our money and how we spend it. As I was once told, if you want to know who is really in control then follow the money trail.

I am a free black man and that gives me the freedom to discuss topics that many of my peers either cannot or will not discuss—at least not in public. I ran away from Massa's plantation many years ago and since I am emancipated, I will say the things that the slaves would like to say, but maybe they can't. I used to be a slave. I used to be on the plantation, so I understand.

Keep in mind that I am not dissing people who are still on the plantation, but I am saying I think you'll be much happier if you get the hell out. Like many people, I got to the threshold where I just could not take it anymore. People were driving me crazy. The way they're treating me was wrong. It was also unethical.

Not only is it unfair, but it's just unbelievable. I think that might be a better phrase, as opposed to just unfair. I almost want to say unfair and unbelievable because as black people, we've grown accustomed to a few things.

We've grown accustomed to all forms of blatant disrespect. In fact, I recently wrote an article on financialjuneteenth.com where I literally went down a list of 15 ways that black people are economically bullied by racist white people. One of the ways that we have become the victims of this is through our representation in mainstream media.

What I don't understand is why we have allowed the media and popular culture to become springboards for black culture.

This has led to the worse kind of bullying. People are economically bullied because, first of all, your kids are brainwashed from birth by media, by the educational system, etc. These are things that you think that you don't have any control over.

But, you do. Black parents who love their children are capable of making sure that their children get an adequate education; furthermore, their children don't have to be subjected to the images that prance across their screens that keep them in subordinate roles.

Then you look at the other forms of disrespect that you see in media. I was talking to a scholar once and he said, "Yeah. Well, you know, I wanted to be mainstream and it didn't work out." I said, "Well, I mean, think about that term mainstream." I said, "You know, I'm not mainstream, but you can't tell me I'm not successful."

You can't tell me that I have not been more successful as a scholar than pretty much every single scholar I've ever met in my entire life other than maybe Cornel West and Michael Eric Dyson. I'm not mainstream. I don't want to be mainstream.

So I said, when you use terms like 'mainstream', you have to be really careful because what you're doing is relegating many black people to the back of the metaphoric bus. It is almost like using the term 'minority'. I don't know if anybody still uses that terminology—maybe if you're over the age of 35 you heard the word minority used a lot, maybe even if you are over the age of 30. But it too was problematic because it connoted powerlessness when in fact, people of a color, on a global level, are the vast majority. We are mot minorities; in fact, we are the majority and powerful.

There is something that always made me cringe when I hear words like mainstream, minority, and diversity. It just seems so lame and watered down, and it is intended to make you feel tiny. Like, I'm a minority. I don't want to do that. I'm a man. I'm a grown ass man. I'm a human being.

I'm not a minority.

Words have power and the words that we are often fed about ourselves from mainstream media are not empowering. There's study after study that says literally one word versus another one affects how you think about yourself and others.

For example, I've read something recently about a diet study. It suggested that if someone is on a diet and somebody offers him some chocolate cake, he might say, "I can't eat chocolate cake". Another person, who's on the same diet, is also offered a slice of chocolate cake. That person says, "I don't eat chocolate cake or I choose not to eat chocolate cake."

Did you know that the person who says that "I don't eat chocolate cake" is far more likely to stay on their diet than the person who says, "I can't eat chocolate cake"?

Because the person who says "I can't" is referring to some magical external force that's not allowing him to do certain things, and it makes it that much more difficult for him to deny the things that he wants because he feels that he's being forbidden from getting what they want.

Whereas the person who says, "I do not eat chocolate cake or I choose not to eat chocolate cake" feels empowered because he feels a sense of power coming from internal mechanisms as opposed to the external.

Do you understand? Now listen to yourselves as black people. Listen to how you talk about racial oppression.

I'm going to ask you this. How many of you all have ever heard a black person say, "Well, you know, Dr. Boyce, we could get more done, but you know, they won't let us do this?" Or, "White folks won't allow us to have that"?

Think about what you're saying to yourself. You're disempowering yourself. You're effectively saying, "I don't have any power over my environment. I am a product of my environment as opposed to the other language, which might imply that your environment is a product of you."

In fact, I've had this debate recently. I've been going back and forth about black wealth with my two of my good friends, Yvette Carnell and Antonio Moore.

I hear Yvette say, "Black wealth . . . we're so far behind and we can't get it done without government help." I'm just walking in there like 'uh-huh' keeping my Ph.D. in finance close to the chest—I keep it nearby so you all know my Ph.D. is real.

I have a 144 page dissertation that I wrote on investing that says that we can build black wealth. We can do this. Now it's not me calling somebody ignorant and saying, oh, you wrong and you stupid. No. I'm not doing all of that. I'm not doing any of that at all. I certainly wouldn't do that to Yvette Carnell because she's probably smarter than me. I think Yvette is one of the smartest human beings on this freaking planet, but on this issue I was like, "Uh-huh, we ain't doing this. We're not using words and phrases like 'we can't' because that's not going to help you."

It never helps you to believe that you have no control over your situation. Let me tell you why. Let me give you another study that helps you understand this. Some scientists studied depression in rats. They planned to measure whether a rat is depressed by the amount of serotonin in its brain.

They took the group of rats and gave them electrical shocks. They just kept shocking them over and over. They gave one group of rats an out. They gave them the ability to control their environment. They had a lever they could pull. If they pulled the level then it would make the shocks stop.

The other rats had no lever; they had no control. The only way the shocks would stop is if the experiment would stop shocking them, so they would just sit and say, we can't do anything about it because the master is going to keep shocking us. We're just going to wait for someone to save us or give us guidance and make us better.

Interestingly, do you know that the rats that had no control over their environment actually were more depressed than the rats that had control over their environment?

My point here is that relinquishing control of your environment, or relinquishing your own ability to shape your outcomes, literally will cause depression. It literally leads to millions of black people feeling like everything is just hopeless. Our attitudes and mindsets shape how we respond to our situations.

In psychological terms, it is called a self-fulfilling prophecy. I will say that for us as black people, it does you no good, no good to walk around saying that you don't control your environment, that you have no say in your environment.

I'm going to believe I have control over my environment even if I don't have control over my environment or the people in it. It doesn't mean I'm not going to accept help or help others if I am in a position to do so.

It doesn't mean I'm not going to hold you responsible for what you might have done to shape my environment. It doesn't mean I'm not going to go to the white man and be like, hey, look. You know what you did to my people?

Every time I speak in front of white people, the white people get mad. Every time. I spoke in front of a group of white bankers, white male bankers, and it was a freaking disaster.

It was one of those situations which was also sad because it was a community organization that had received some white savior money to do some work in the hood. I respect it. I mean, I wanted the organization to get their money, but when they invited me, I was thinking: *You do understand that I'm going to be who I am no matter what the environment is?* I always ask people when I see something that's a little too mainstream; in fact, I'll talk to the person who's organizing the event to make sure they understand that I won't dilute my message.

When I spoke to this group of white male bankers, literally five or six of them got up and walked out of the room. The minute I started talking about reparations and telling the truth about reparations, they walked out of the damn room. What really says to me is that America is a divided country. It's a long way from being an equitable country because you got people out here that don't even want to hear the truth. We have people out here that want to penalize you for being honest.

On different occasions, I have actually said, " Are you sure you want me to come in there? Are you sure ... because I'll get you fired. I'll try my best not to. I'll try my best to be polite, but I won't get up there and lie. I'm going to battle a white man. I'm not going to deny what has happened to our people, so make sure you're ready for this."

I, specifically, recall a time when I spoke at a Black Chamber of Commerce event. The organizer told me that he wanted me to "bring it 100%." I replied, "We're going to bring it?" He said, "Just bring it."

We brought it and it was great. The black people were standing up and cheering. The white people sat down and they kind of politely clapped.

That speaks to a big part of the reason that I wanted to have this chapter in the book. You have to think about the kind of Negros they're putting in front of you on mainstream media.

When you see black people being heavily promoted by white corporations, or Jewish corporations, you need to ask yourself, why are they picking that person as opposed to somebody else who might be just as talented or more talented? What is it about this black person's willingness to support the agenda of their boss that has made that person the favorite Negro?

One great example of this is Lee Daniels. Lee Daniels is responsible for the show *Empire*. It's a beautiful show. It's well-done. The cinematography is just magnificent, but there is a problem—actually, several of them.

I watched two episodes when I was in Africa just because that's what they had on. I was like, well, if I'm going to talk about *Empire*, I need to go ahead and watch it. You know what happened when I watched *Empire*?

I am not going to lie. I started to like it. What that tells me is that poison is addictive.

Poison can taste better than fruits and vegetables if you're not careful. Literally, I was watching it and I thought that it was a good show. I wondered what the next episode would entail. I said to myself: "Wait. Stop, Boyce. Don't do it. Don't do it."

A lot of people will say, but Dr. Boyce, how can you criticize something if you don't watch it? You need to watch it so you can critique it. I'm like, no.

Sometimes I don't want to watch too much of it because I know that I'm going to like it. I know there's a reason that millions of people already like this mess and I don't want to know what that reason is.

It's like drugs and alcohol addiction. You can' get hooked if you never try either one. I don't drink and people say, how do you know if you don't like it if you don't drink it?

I know I'm going to like it because I have alcoholics in my family. We have an alcoholism gene that runs through our family and I've seen a lot of black men in my family get ruined from drinking too much, so I already know if I start drinking and I get a taste for liqueur, I'm going to be a drinker. I will probably be a big drinker. I don't want to be an alcoholic, so I avoid it altogether, just like avoiding a pretty girl.

Sometimes as a man, especially as a heterosexual black man from the South, when you see a girl that's real pretty and you know she's too good for you, you might not want to look at her. I don't want to be near her. Just go away. I'll even look down. I'll literally look like I'm looking at the sun. Sounds illogical, right?

I'm not going to stare at you directly because my masculine instincts might take over and I might be aiming for something that's very bad for me. But, you can't outsmart your human nature. You can't outsmart Mother Nature. You can't outsmart God. You can't outsmart instincts. You can't outsmart pheromones.

Pheromones are the things that human beings release that make them attractive to each other, so at the end of the day, as much as we want to think as human beings that we're so elevated above animals, we are not. Don't believe me? Go listen to Professor Sapolsky at Stanford University who's a great behavioral anthropologist.

He will tell you that 95% of the human brain is actually equal to an animal's brain. Animal brains and human brains are 95% alike. There's that last 5% - the prefrontal cortex - that allows you to think in a different, more complex way. It allows you to be logical, and it allows you to play chess and do calculus and build skyscrapers and run stupid presidential campaigns, and whatever it is that we do as humans that makes us feel different.

At end of the day, we are all animals. My point is that we can't deny our humanity. We also have to understand that there are people out there who work to get us addicted to poison. There is so much on TV that it is almost impossible to watch if you want to avoid the toxicity.

There's no redeeming quality to it whatsoever. Even the people who create the garbage won't let their own kids watch this stuff. The execs over at BET don't have their own kids getting into all this, watching the BET Awards, and internalizing the culture.

But they'll sprinkle all that nonsense on the hood and let the people in the hood get shot up and everything else because you're sprayed in this toxic culture. They don't care because they're going off to the suburbs. They aren't in the hood. They are in gated communities.

We have to think about the coonery that's being put in front of us on TV. In fact, one of the things that I talked to my team about, and people have been pushing me to do is a TV show. Somebody has said that I should create a TED Talk platform for black people. The idea is to host an event where you get smart black people to go on stage and present more complex and positive presentations of Black culture and Black people.

That is a great idea. That's a beautiful idea, but you know what? The problem is you got a lot of Negros who got a lot of ideas, but don't know how to fund them. Furthermore, they are not willing to put up money to make it happen. I'll watch it if it's free, right? There is a budget. It costs money to do this.

My thought is that maybe one day I can come up with a low cost framework that would allow us to elevate those black people who would never get on mainstream TV, those black people that deserve all of the love and accolades and rewards that we give to athletes and entertainers and thuggish rappers and everything else, but they don't get that because mainstream media does not reward black intelligence as much as it rewards straight coonery and ignorance and self-destruction.

Since TV is not a viable option right now, we did come up with a format called *Intellectual Chocolate*. And here's why it is important that we create and support our own media platforms.

We invite smart black people from all walks of life. We

spotlight black people who are intelligent; black people who are the scientists, doctors, lawyers, engineers, professors, activists, authors and everything else that we don't often get to see on mainstream TV.

We're going to put the interviews on my YouTube channel. My YouTube channel, youtube.com/drboycewatkins, just passed 40 million views on the channel. This way, we can do our part to shine a spotlight on those black people who are toiling away and quietly building the future.

The black person who is sitting in a lab and helping to cure cancer deserves to be seen and heard more so than a person who's claim to fame is being a reality TV star. There's also that black person who might be the astrophysicist who discovered the planet that nobody knew about or that black person who is doing amazing activism in their community that nobody is celebrating because we are so focused on the negativity.

I go to a lot of cities and you see people doing the best work, and they get no support because people are addicted to poison. They're addicted to instant gratification, so they're more likely to run to the club than they are to actually run to the rally.

Perhaps the story of LeBron James illustrates this further. When LeBron James and the Cleveland Cavaliers won the championship, there were millions of people in the street. When Tamir Rice was shot nobody was out there rallying for him and his family.

A few people were mad, but there should have been just as many people out there talking about Tamir Rice as there were talking about LeBron James winning the championship. LeBron should have been one of the first people to have pushed that to the forefront of the national media, but unfortunately, I guess the pressure got too be too much. I understand.

I'm not dissing LeBron. I think LeBron actually does better than most athletes, but part of the reason that he stands out so much is because the bar is set so damn low. We just expect so little from our athletes and entertainers because they are so committed to supporting white supremacist systems that we don't expect them to have simple human decency when it comes to dealing with the tragedies that are affecting our community so much.

Every athlete should be a Colin Kaepernick. Colin should not be standing out by himself and be a lone ranger, and the one guy who suddenly made it cool to be conscious. There should be 200 athletes who are just like this.

Maybe if they were exposed to positive media, positive, strong black intelligent media then they would realize how much they're wasting by getting on the gridiron every week in front of millions of people and showing white people that they only know how to catch a damn football.

So *Intellectual Chocolate* (intellectualchocolate.com) is our effort to try to help with that. We can't wait for others to celebrate smart black people; everybody needs to celebrate and hear about how great we are.

I just want there to be a place for smart black people because what happens now is that smart black people who want to be out there have to dumb down to appeal to the masses or appeal to mainstream media.

I can't tell you how many times I might go to a radio station and have them literally encourage me to keep it simple. Some have said, "Dr. Boyce, we want you to talk in quick sound bites and don't talk about things that are too complicated."

Instead of us being minimized and silenced and instead of taking our biggest intellectual giants and crushing their faces into the ground to make them small, I say we take everybody and we stretch them and make them all stand tall. It is not a competition. I say that we take intellectualism and we make it the coolest, sexiest, most amazing thing on the planet, hence the name.

I believe that the way we can do this is through the ownership of strong black media that reaches lots of people. Right now, my YouTube channel gets only about three million views a month, but in a year, that'll be up to five or six million. Also on Facebook, we can reach two to three million Facebook fans on all of the different pages that we own and have partnerships with. If you check the numbers, MSNBC, and most of their shows only reach 200 or 300,000 people, so we have the ability to create black media, but we have to think creatively about what that looks like.

The recent example of Tamron Hall being replaced at *The Today Show* is yet another reminder why we have to be power and culture brokers. This requires having the financial leverage to walk away when we are treated in an unfair or discriminatory manner by our employer. We see this too often with Black people in mainstream media in particular

Since media can be defined as the ability of one person to communicate with another, something doesn't have to be TV to be considered effective. It doesn't have to be on the radio to reach the masses. It doesn't have to be in print. It's all about having a strong, great mind.

Because I understand the power of media, I ask you to share all of the time. I'm always saying please share, please subscribe, please share, please subscribe, please like, please do whatever. I ask you to do that because I'm thinking that if we keep pushing then we can build this media out, stretch it out, and make it reach even more people.

Share it with your cousins. If you've got friends with big pages, ask them to put it on their page. Stretch it out so that everybody can see this because what I find is that when people are exposed to these ideas, they usually gravitate toward them. Even black people who do stupid stuff like embrace liberal ideas, extreme liberal ideas or become Republicans, or go out and do stuff that doesn't make any sense like support white supremacist institutions, a lot of times, they do it because they don't know that alternative views and platforms are out here.

They don't know that there's a place where you can be smart and black and that's a cool thing.

A lot of rappers I know are very smart people, but they dumb themselves down, which irritates the hell out of me. There's no bigger plague in society than a smart rapper who makes himself stupid so he can fit in, so 2 Chainz, I'm talking to you.

I'm talking to 2 Chainz. I don't care about him bragging about, "I went to college and I was a straight A student, this and that and the other." If you were a straight A student then act like it.

Why would you be a straight A student, a scholar, and an intellect, but then do everything you can to act like a dumb ass n%**@^? That doesn't make any sense. He is brilliantly ignorant, literally, brilliantly ignorant.

What does that mean? Being brilliantly ignorant means that because your social intelligence is so high, you need to adapt to your environment in order to fit in. Because his social intelligence is so high, you will see 2 Chainz literally having the ability to emulate ignorant people. You saw that with Trinidad James.

Remember Trinidad James? "Gold all in my chain, gold all in my ring, gold all in my watch." Do you remember that?

I went to the Breakfast Club the day after Trinidad James had just left. Everybody was just raving over how smart he was. Like, you know, he's really intelligent. If you get to know him, he's very smart.

I'm like, what good is it if he's intelligent if he doesn't show anyone? The world does not judge you based on what you are. The world judges you by what you do and by what you show.

Yet, our community eats this up. We idolize these figures and continue to make them and their sponsors rich.

We buy into this. Yet, we need to better understand how our power and our money (via sponsorships and advertisements) are literally being given away to people who could care less about the preservation of the black community.

We are being conditioned on a daily basis. For example, if I tell you that I'm a good person, why would you believe me? Maybe it is because I love to help old ladies and protect children. I take care of puppies and donate to the poor. Would you also think that I am weak?

But then, let's say that I went out and hurt eight people. Instead of showing you that I'm a nice person, I might cuss out people and disrespect women, and call them Bs and Hs, or do other horrible things to anybody I see.

I then try to convince you that those horrible behaviors are not really a reflection of me. They are just an act. I'm only saying and doing these things because people don't respect a man if he's nice, good, or helpful.

What's going to have the greater impact? The things I do and say; the things you see; or the things you don't see? I would just say that if somebody said that Trinidad James is an entrepreneur, and rappers often tailor their product to their audience, that's still not an excuse. If we follow that logic then drug dealers are entrepreneurs.

Can you justify somebody who deals heroin in your neighborhood, or next door to you? Is it ok because he's just an entrepreneur? He's just tailoring his product to the customer, right?

No, this is no excuse. I know hit-men, I've literally known hit-men who were just entrepreneurs. I'm just a businessman. I murder people for money. You can't use that as an excuse. They have a term in economics and I want you to write this down because I want you to dig deeper into this term. It's called externalities. Externalities are basically anything that affects the environment that you operate your business in. In other words, it is anything that's outside of the business, or the scope of business.

Imagine if I ran a company and we made really good products, and they were really cheap, but we dumped toxic waste into the river. It polluted the river and people were dying; kids were getting cancer and babies were being born with two heads because we were putting toxic waste into the water supply.

You can't talk about my business model and the success of it without talking about the externalities because I might be making 10 million a year, but I might be causing a billion dollars' worth of damage every year.

White owned networks like BET are pushing poison. Yes, they're trying to do better, so I'm not as hard on BET as I used to be. When I would challenge them, the first thing they would say to me is we're tailoring our product to the audience. This is what the audience wants, so that's what we're giving them.

I refuted that the audience's taste is defined by what they put in front of them. I argued that BET couldn't say that their product was a function of what the audience want. BET created a taste for the ignorant and for the dysfunctional, so they also had to think about their doing to the community. What are your externalities?

They all went to Harvard and Yale so they understood business, but they also understood what the images were doing to our youth. They wouldn't let their kids consume this.

They knew how destructive their programming was, and yet, they pushed it and pedaled it only because it was making them all money, but no one considered the externalities on these neighborhoods where people were emulating the behavior that they saw in the mainstream media.

You cannot talk about any business or any product without thoroughly discussing the externalities of that product's existence.

We know how rap works. Most of the people who buy that stuff are white kids and what they're doing is they're basically using you as a minstrel show or this coon fest. It is an escape for them, I guess, because white people have it so easy.

Don't get me wrong, some white people struggle, but they don't have black people problems, most of them don't. So, since they don't have black people problems, they get to go into this fantasy-mode where they get to see some thugged out black man talking about how many other black men he shot last week or how many baby mamas he has. He can pretend like he throwing money up in the club or how he's shooting someone in the face if he steps on his white shoes. Or he can romanticize how he went to prison and kept it real with all of his tattoos on his face.

Yes, this is laden with every stereotype imaginable—that was my point. How uncomfortable did you feel? Sounds crazy until you think about the fact that our children consume this on a daily basis.

Rappers are getting tattoos on their faces; they walk around with 50 pounds of jewelry, looking like clowns. What are they doing?

They're trying to basically appeal to all of these white people who are buying their stuff. They are trying to say, no, no, no. You liked him because he was thugged out. I'm more thugged out than him. Look, I've got a whole mouth full of gold. He had one gold tooth. I got a whole mouth full of platinum.

I got tear drops to show you how many n#@@$%! I've shot, so I'm the ultimate thug. I'm the one that fulfills your little thug fantasy about what life is like in the hood because it's not real to you.

The reality is that the white consumers of this music have never been on the South side of the Chicago. They have never seen so many people getting shot that little old ladies can't walk down the street safely anymore.

Somebody is dropping off these guns. It's another way that they're making money off of your genocide. But the people who are pushing this music won't have to deal with that real stuff, so they think it's cool and our children think it's fun.

But, it is not fun. It perpetuates self-hatred and degradation. It also creates an overly simplistic representation of Black culture.

It is no different than when we were children and we used to watch karate movies, particularly Bruce Lee movies. We all thought everybody in China knew karate. Watching mafia movies like *The Godfather* made us think that every Italian wanted to be part of the mafia.

This is the supreme power of mainstream media and it reflects its ability to influence how we see groups of people.

The same thing is true for black people. Their fantasy is this whole thug thing and we're exporting the thug culture to the world in exchange for white people's money. Therefore, you have rappers that are going in front of an audience full of white people and will call themselves n^##*^@& on stage and the white people will cheer. The white people will literally cheer in approval.

I saw Snoop Dogg and Dr. Dre. You remember Dr. Dre, right? Dr. Dre is the idiot who gave 70 million dollars to USC. I'm going to talk about this probably for about the next 40 years because I think it was literally one of the dumbest decisions that any human being has ever made in life.

I feel bad if Dre feels bad about it, but I don't feel bad enough to stop saying this because there are literally about 100,000 black youth who would have gotten educated over the next, say, 50 to 100 years who will not be educated because you decided to give your money to a white university that uses 70 million dollars to buy toilet paper.

USC has an endowment that exceeds the endowment of every HBCU in America combined.

Better yet, if you add up the endowment of every HBCU in this country and add it all up in one pile, then you still won't come close to USC's endowment. Why in the world would your dumb black ass go give your money to USC when you have all of these HBCUs that could have taken just a fraction of that money and transformed an entire community?

That's how deep the brainwashing is. That is the poison that occurs. It hits people's brains when you're constantly promoting ignorance in mainstream media.

As black people, my argument is that we should not tolerate it. We should not tolerate it..

When I went to LA and I did an event in South Central, I met people that knew Dre. I knew that he had an issue with an article that I wrote about him. I hated it because I'm friends with certain people who are friends with Dre. I don't like attacking any black person, but I don't know what else to say. Perhaps, someone on his team should have thought that through and advised him differently.

Maybe he'll go give some money to some HBCUs just to shut me up. If he does, I'll go shut up. If he went and gave 10 million to Hampton, or not even Hampton. Hampton is nice, but Hampton has got a lot of rich people. Go give it to Southern University or give it to Dillard University or give it to another school like Clark Atlanta University. I think Clark would really benefit because Clark, unfortunately, gets overshadowed a little bit by Morehouse and Spelman.

The real problem is that whether its BET, or some other affiliate, renting is not owning. When we don't own our own platforms, we can't control the narrative. We also can't control how the revenue is spent and where. Have you ever wondered if any of the proprietors of any of the most popular black TV shows reinvested in black communities? Have they helped black students or provided paid internships?

If you get rich off of black people, you owe it to black people to put resources, financial and otherwise, back into our community.

We're all talking about these issues, but we just don't have the media platforms to really get that, and other, message out, so as black people we end up feeling a little bit stuck.

You have the angry underbelly of people who are looking at these celebrities doing these really stupid things, and we're just mad about it and we don't have any way to speak out about it.

As a person who has a little bit of media savvy, I don't have the resources of media conglomerates like ABC, CBS and NBC, but I'm building now. Every little channel we have reaches black people.

There's not a city in this country I can go to now where a brother or a sister doesn't recognize me, so it must be working. Every bit of media that I build now is being built so that in two generations, my grandchildren will be running a multi-billion dollar media empire.

What you have to understand is that every single great institution in this country started as a mom and pop shop. Almost all of them did, almost every single one of them. If it's not every one of them, it's the vast majority. Maybe some started off with big financing, but a lot of them started off with nothing more than a dream, even as other people made fun of them or chimed in, "Oh, that's no big deal. Let it go."

What I learned a long time ago is don't ever piss on your own dream. Never underestimate what you might be creating. If you create it now, you will reap the benefits. I'm sacrificing my life for what I want my grandchildren to have. I don't have a life. I didn't get married. I had a daughter. I didn't have more kids. I sacrificed my life for this because I know that the benefits are going to be life altering for those whom I love.

Sure, I get a few of the benefits, but they're going to be great for my grandkids who will have something that is powerful. Maybe one day, my grandkids and great-grandkids will be able to brag, "My granddaddy was Dr. Boyce Watkins." You got to buy into something that's bigger than you.

You can't just buy into getting a paycheck next Friday. Your life is worth more than just that paycheck that you just sacrificed all those hours to get. Ask yourself, what am I buying into that's bigger than me? What am I buying into that will benefit children that are not yet born? What am I doing right now that's going to be around, that's going to have impact on my community 200 years from today or my family 200 years from today?

Think about how many things we're doing right now that are the result of sacrifices people made 200 years ago. Think about it and then ask yourself, what are you willing to fight for? What in the hell are you willing to fight for?

You have black people that fought in the Civil War so that you could be free, and they died. They didn't get any of the benefits of their sacrifice, but imagine if they had thought the way that many of us think. If I can't get nothing from it, then I'm not going to do it. What if they had thought the same way? Guess what? We'd still be enslaved. We'd still be slaves right now.

If you can't name something you're willing to fight for, or at least sacrifice for, at an extensive level, then you have not yet lived. You are living in a cage. You are not an asset to your family nor to your community. You're not even an asset to yourself. You're probably wasting your life. You're wasting your life, so find something that you believe in.

Just like I believe that *Intellectual Chocolate* will change the way that black people are represented. The interviewer, Dr. Johari Shuck, will highlight individuals in the community who are doing amazing things, who are not getting the attention that they deserve.

The concept of fighting for freedom or fighting in a revolutionary scenario, means that when something doesn't exist, you have to create your own. We don't have to wait for others to create jobs for us, provide us with platforms. We definitely cannot wait media outlets, or mainstream media, to tell our stories for us—we see what that's led to.

We have the ability, the fortitude, and the sheer numbers to create and sustain our own jobs, communities, and media outlets. There was a time when a good job was staying 30 years at the same place, retiring with a pension, and passing down one's home. Now, we must think about the images and culture that we are passing on to the next generation.

The next time you turn a channel or listen to music, ask yourself: Who really owns this image? This sounds? This culture? Today, we know that there is more to us as a culture and it all starts with you, right now.

CHAPTER 9

LET'S TALK ABOUT MONEY IN REAL TERMS: AN INTERVIEW WITH THE BREAKFAST CLUB

One of the things that is very important to me is to make sure that I am able to share the importance of financial literacy across platforms and with diverse audiences of black people. The Breakfast Club is an influential morning radio program that is based in New York City, but its reach is worldwide. When sharing gems of wisdom, I try to present information in a way that the audience will be able to take away not just information, but strategies for application.

In this segment, we have what I'd like to call a real discussion about money, entrepreneurship, and investing. To maintain the authenticity, we have not edited the language. As you read through it, I want you to think about the various ways that multigenerational conversations, partnerships, and wealth-building can change the life trajectories of black people everywhere.

DJ Envy: Morning everybody it's DJ Envy, Angela

	Yee, Charlamagne Tha God. We are the Breakfast Club. We have a special guest in the building this morning.
Charlamagne:	That's right.
DJ Envy:	Dr. Boyce Watkins. Good Morning Sir.
Dr. Boyce W.:	What's happening brother, how you doing?
DJ Envy:	How you doing today?
Dr. Boyce W.:	Oh everything is good.
Charlamagne:	Long time pal of mine, you know we've been having a conversation for the past two weeks about financial, I call it illiteracy. You know, ever since Mrs. Damon Dash left. It sparks up a good conversation in our community just about finances and entrepreneurship.
Dr. Boyce W.:	Investing.
Charlamagne:	Investing and self-empowerment so I wanted to reach out to a financial expert that I know. Dr. Boyce Watkins. Now for people who aren't familiar tell them why you're a financial expert.
Dr. Boyce W.:	Well I'm a Ph.D. in finance and I taught finance for about 20 years at the University of Kentucky, Indiana University, Syracuse University, etc. I know a lot about money. I know what it's like to not have any money. I

used to really want money. That's why I majored in finance. I wasn't even really supposed to go to college. I figured if I studied money and learn about money somebody will pay me money to talk about money. But then I really also learned how money can be used as a tool not just to liberate you, but it can also enslave you. We have a lot of multimillionaires in our community that are scared of their own shadow, that are just afraid of everything, afraid to be controversial, etc., and I think sometimes we look at money in the wrong way.

Money is powerful like fire or like a drug. Like fire can either cook your food and keep you warm, or it can burn you and your family alive. A drug can either heal you and make you better, or it can turn you into an addict. So that relationship with money I think is important because most of us think about money several times a day every day.

Charlamagne: And you wrote several books on finance as well.

Dr. Boyce W.: Yeah. I wrote a book called Black American Money. I have another book coming out called It Takes a Village to Raise the Bar: A New Paradigm for Black America, it's basically talking about ways to think about money and ways that money can really be the next step in our civil rights movement

	because if you have political power without any economic power, that's kind of like having a driver's license but not having a car. You're not going to go anywhere unless somebody else wants to give you a ride and then at that point you're still only going to go where they want to take you.
Charlamagne:	Gotcha.
DJ Envy:	Now question. Damon Dash. You mentioned that earlier. What did you think of Damon Dash's interview?
Dr. Boyce W.:	You know what, I -
Charlamagne:	You described him as a breath of fresh air.
Dr. Boyce W.:	Yes. You know what? I liked, here's what I liked about Dame. I liked the energy that Dame comes with. To me, I think that so many black men have been so emasculated economically and it's not something that just recently started happening; it's been happening for hundreds of years, that I like the idea of just having a call to manhood and kind of saying, "Look, we can do better." Sometimes, like you think about it on the football field, your coach there motivates you to play. Sometimes he's going to punk you out. Like, "You were playing like a bitch. Get up! You need to win!" But the thing with Dame that's interesting is

that he's a little bit like an economic version of a Harriet Tubman, you know, "I'm a get these slaves off the plantation, or I'm a shoot you if I have to." But we all understand that in order to escape the plantation you have to have a plan, right? To go to war you have to have a battle strategy. But not having a strategy in here right away does not give you an excuse to not fight. So that's what I like about Dame. I think Dame started a conversation.

Charlamagne: Yeah.

DJ Envy: Yeah

Dr. Boyce W.: We weren't really talking about this kind of thing two or three weeks ago, so I'm glad he did it.

DJ Envy: But its deadly. It's very deadly and it could hurt a lot of our audience, especially a lot of youth.

Angela Yee: But there were a lot of different things that were said. Some things that we may agree with, some things we may not agree with.

DJ Envy: _____ some of Dame's rhetoric.

DJ Envy: Do you enjoy the safety and security of a job every day? Pride in the activity _____

DJ Envy: Now let me ask you a question. There are millions of people out there that don't have

	that opportunity and have a boss every day -
DJ Envy:	We all have that opportunity.
Charlamagne:	Have a boss every day. So you're basically saying that because they have a boss there's no pride in it?
DJ Envy:	I think because people on the radio tell people it's okay to have a boss. They don't understand that they could have more. It's just a pride you should have in ownership.
Charlamagne:	How do you get to that platform? -
DJ Envy:	Opening your own money up and investing it in yourself.
Charlamagne:	Well that's the reason why we set up the platform so they don't have to do anything.
DJ Envy:	You have a boss. How can a man say he has a boss and be proud?
Charlamagne:	Okay, no pride in having a job. Having a boss is like calling another man daddy. And how can you have a boss and be proud?
Dr. Boyce W.:	I think it's okay to have a boss. Everybody has some kind of a boss on some level. Like the interview you did with Andy, I think is his name.
Charlamagne:	Andrew.

Dr. Boyce W.: Yeah Andrew. Even if you own your own business you have someone that you have to answer to. Right, every day when I get up and I'm motivated, I'm answering to the boss that lives inside of me, that's saying, "If you don't get off your butt you're not gonna achieve your goals." So everybody has some sort of boss. The question is whether or not you're being pimped by your life. Whether or not someone is ... is your boss to the point where you don't feel free? You don't have any degrees of freedom in your life. You feel stuck in your own existence. I think in that situation you have to make a change.

Because here's the thing, and a lot of people don't get this. If you work for me, and I'm the reason that your children can eat every day, I'm the reason that your wife has a roof over her head, you're not really the man of your house. I'm the man of your house. And so I think that having someone you answer to is okay, but if you can somehow shift your situation where everything is a partnership where you have options. For example, one question you can answer is do you have F you money? If somebody on your job calls you the N word or disrespects you or you just hate your job, do you have enough put aside? Do you have enough other options so you can walk in and say F you, I'm out? If you can't really do that, then I would say you have to adjust something in your life.

	Just because you're committed to something doesn't mean you don't have options.
DJ Envy:	Right.
Dr. Boyce W.:	So is there no pride in having a boss? I don't think we can agree with a statement like that per se. But there's just dignity in working hard, no matter what. But I do think that if you are being pimped by your life, you have to make an adjustment.
Angela Yee:	Like I say to some of my friends who might complain all the time, "I hate my job. I hate my boss. I hate this." I'm like, well you can't complain about it for too long. You gotta do something about it. In that case if you really hate it and it's not what you wanna do, at some point, instead of complaining for years and years and years, you gotta get up, and you know, and do something. Change it, get a new job, and make some more opportunities.
Dr. Boyce W.:	Yeah absolutely. I think what we have to embrace, is the idea of ownership. I want to believe the best about what Dame was trying to do. And I think that this is a conversation that has to be had with a community. Not with one person leading this, me, him or anybody else. All these ideas have to be laid out on the table. But I think that what we need to really consider is the idea and importance of building things. We need a

nation of builders. That's why I love Louis Farrakhan for example. He's one of my favorite black leaders because he build his stuff. He didn't climb up somebody else's tree, he planted the seed and grew his own tree and climbed to the top of that.

Charlamagne: The baton was passed.

Dr. Boyce W.: Right the baton was passed, but at the same time, there's a building mentality within the Nation of Islam that I think we can all learn from. It does not mean that you don't form partnerships, it doesn't mean there's no pride in working for other people per se. I can't sign on for something like that but I do think that we have to resurrect the pride of building as opposed to just borrowing. Because what we don't understand sometimes is that ... I'm really talking about people of color right now. A lot of the stuff that's out here, it really wasn't built for us. It wasn't. These corporations were creating by other people of other ethnicities a hundred years ago and we get in there and we somehow become disappointed and surprised when we're treated differently because we're black and we don't get the same opportunities. But you can't really move in somebody else's house and then expect to be able to shift around the furniture. It just does not really work. I think taking that pride and building your own house and being proud of that, right?

	Because think about this, if you start your own business, you're not going to be ballin, for a while, if ever.
Angela Yee:	Right.
Dr. Boyce W.:	Right? But you have to realize you can't judge the quality of the tree by the size of the seed. Every tree's going to start tiny and you grow that. You grow that over several generations. Even large companies like the Ford Motor Company. If you look at the history of a company like that it started off as a tiny seed. It was nothing. Now it's massive and I think we have to ask ourselves, not about what's happening in 2015, but what's going to be happening in 2115 with our grandchildren, great-grandchildren, great-great grandchildren. What are you passing on?
Charlamagne:	I think we're playing those themes now. I think this is the first generation of wealth for black people. You know the Civil Rights Act was founded in 1964, we were still in segregation 51 years ago.
Dr. Boyce W.:	Yeah but I tell you man, I don't even know if black people have that much wealth.
Charlamagne:	Are we creating the first round of billionaires?
Dr. Boyce W.:	You're seeing some of the black elite doing

	extremely well. I don't think that the black lower and middle class are doing all that well.
Charlamagne:	Won't it take time though?
Dr. Boyce W.:	It does.
DJ Envy:	One thing I do agree with. As a kid growing up I didn't learn about being an entrepreneur or investing. My parents ... they ... my pops was a police officer my mom worked at Garden Life Insurance. They didn't instill that in me. I instill it in my kids cause I was a little different. But the problem I have with Dame, when I said it's deadly, is you telling these kids, "Don't have a boss. You get out there and do it." And see the problem with Dame is if you listen to Dame or you listen to past interviews or you listen to the Holmes record, you see that they started their business from illegal-
Dr. Boyce W.:	Illegal activity
DJ Envy:	Illegal activity. So you're encouraging kids, "Well I don't have a boss. I started like him." No. I went to college. I went to high school, got my degree, I went to college, got my degree. I started working, saved my money and that's how I built my empire. And you're telling kids, "Well, you shouldn't do that." And that was my problem because a lot of kids listen.

Charlamagne:	Well he did say he sells tee shirts now. You know [crosstalk 00:09:35]
DJ Envy:	Well where you get the money to sell tee shirts. As a drug dealer you [inaudible 00:09:41] some weed.
Charlamagne:	You gotta have some capital.
DJ Envy:	You gotta have some capital. And the way y get capital is having a job and put money on the side. And I don't see nothing wrong with having a boss.
Dr. Boyce W.:	Well let me tell you. Look I agree with you. I think we can agree on that for sure. And one thing I'll supplement with, and it's not really a matter of fighting about it one way or the other. There's a book called The Hundred Dollar Start Up. Which basically explains how you can start a business for under a hundred bucks. I know this type of stuff works because I started something with my brother for about 700 dollars a couple years ago. We made a quarter million dollars within two years. Right? So just from that one business. And the thing was, if I hadn't of been thinking, "Okay, what can I create? What can I generate?" I never would have done that.
	Sometimes we get caught in thinking that a job is something that someone is supposed to give us. A job is also something you can

	create. It doesn't mean you have to do it, but one thing I do say, is I think every parent who cares about their kids should teach their child how to have their own business even if they go work for somebody else. It doesn't mean that you have to be an entrepreneur. Everybody isn't built for that.
DJ Envy:	Right.
Dr. Boyce W.:	But what I would say is, either run something, or invest in something. So for example. If I got together with three other people and let's say the other three didn't want to be entrepreneurs. They didn't have the time, they want to keep their jobs, well everybody comes up with say, two thousand dollars. You pull together that six. I get my 25 percent of the company but with equities because I've got free time. So I'm going to run the company because I have the expertise and the free time. You guys are investors, therefore we all own something.
Charlamagne:	But were you get that money from though?
Dr. Boyce W.:	Well if you're working. If you got a job you can come up with 2,000 bucks over time. It may take you a year to save it or whatever. But you can come up with that. We invest in so many other things. People always say that black people can't really create jobs and I don't think that's true. We create a lot of jobs for other people. When we're spending all

this money on these brands and all this other stuff that we do we're not thinking where that money is going. I think that is the problem. We're sort of letting our power escape. Money is your power and you cannot give your power away because at the end of the day you will be powerless.

Angela Yee: I just saw recent that an article about an entrepreneur. He was working at a phone store right, where a lot of the phones that they don't sell. They don't have anything that they can do with it. It might be some old phones and they just laying around. He started his own business that turned into a billion dollar business where he would get those phones that they didn't sell, and he would sell them to companies that maybe you know, at your job, everybody gets a cell phone that your company gives to you. He was selling those phones that they didn't use at the store, he was like the go-between person selling them to companies that had to give their employees cell phones, and he turned it into a billion dollar business. Just from working at this cell phone store.

Dr. Boyce W.: It's all ideas. It's all about ideas.

Angela Yee: And I don't think he needed much money to start that. He just started mediating those because he saw a need, he saw that there was this overflow of phones, and he saw that there were companies that needed to give employees phones and didn't want to spend a whole lot of money so he just merged the two ideas together.

Dr. Boyce W.: Yeah, there you go. The thing is that to come up with those ideas you have to have a certain kind of spirit. You have to have, you know, really creating a job for yourself it's a little bit like the difference between somebody who thinks that they can eat if the grocery store has food or if a restaurant serves them versus somebody who says, "Well actually, if worse comes to worse I can grow my own food. I can cook my own food. I'm not going to starve.' So you should never starve to death because somebody would not bring food to you.

Angela Yee: Right.

Dr. Boyce W.: You should know how to create your own food. I think it's an idea in terms of creating opportunities. It's about building the entrepreneurial spirit which starts with taking pride in that. I have so much more respect when I hear about young brothers that don't have much, who say, "I own something. I'm building something." Than I have for people who say, "Oh I work for such and such corporation. I'm making a lot of money." It doesn't mean that both people aren't accomplished, but I really think we have to build. I really think that this affects us politically and socioeconomically in the sense that people can ... people don't respect you when you're always begging for something. Malcolm X talk about that. He said, "Look, as long as you are begging for jobs from businesses that you do not own, you will always be severely unemployed."

If you look at the unemployment disparity, in 1965- 1964 when Malcolm was saying this, till 2015, it hasn't changed that much.

Charlamagne: And that's why Dame was telling people there's no pride in having a job. Why are you complaining about being unemployed -

Dr. Boyce W.: I think that you can be proud if you are a proud person but I think that at the end of the day, you have to figure out what you're comfortable with, what you can live with. Let's be real. Racism is stressful for people. When they're dealing with ... There's an angry black middle class of people who did all the right things, they went to school, they worked hard, they got these corporate jobs, and they are pissed off because they know they're being treated unfairly but they don't feel that they have any options.

Angela Yee: Right.

Dr. Boyce W.: Many case studies have shown that this affects your health. For a man, it kills your testosterone. People get cancer, I mean people get sick off of this stuff. So my

	things is you have to find a way to liberate yourself and restore your manhood. I think it affects our families because I think that black women have a hard time really respecting black men the way they should because many of us have been so beaten down by the society. We don't know what to do.
Charlamagne:	We're not in a position of power.
Dr. Boyce W.:	Right. I'm not saying there's some sort of fundamental flaw in who we are, I'm saying that maybe we need to resurrect some ideas that can restore that power mainly. There was nothing better that happened in my life it terms of dealing with racism, than when I figured out how to start my own stuff. It made me stronger, it made me prouder, it made me more courageous. I've got into this crazy ... When I worked at Syracuse University I was dealing with all this racism and all this stuff, and I got into this big fight with Bill O'Reilly about something.
Charlamagne:	I remember that.
Dr. Boyce W.:	Remember that? He made a joke about lynching with Michelle Obama and I didn't like that so we got into it and whatever. Well he worked really hard to get my fired. I'm talking about really hard to the point where multimillion dollar donors are saying, "Where not going to give any money to your

school because you've got racist." You know how O'Reilly do.

Charlamagne: Is that why you stepped down?

Dr. Boyce W.: That played a big part in it, yes. They only defining factor is terms of whether or not I could stand by what I said versus apologizing to something I did not do was, whether or not my financial situation was right -

Charlamagne: The F you money.

Dr. Boyce W.: Yes, when you're F you money is right, you have the ability to be a little bold. I'm not more courageous than other people. I just checked my money, my bank account, checked my businesses and said, "Okay, if I get fired, I'm going to be okay."

Charlamagne: Right.

Dr. Boyce W.: You understand? So that's the idea. The thing is, it wasn't just my situation, I think it's a microcosm of what so many of us experience every day. Just make sure you've got options for yourself. If you got options I think you're going to be all right.

Charlamagne: I want to ask you about what you said. If I misquote you let me know. You said that a man is not a man if he has a job that ... you're not the man of your house, the boss is the man of your house?

Dr. Boyce W.: You know what? I will say this: it is fundamentally flawed for you to depend on the descendants of your historical oppressors to get the things that you need in order to survive.

Charlamagne: The reason I ask you that is because, somebody like you. You went to school. You busted your ass, you get your degree. You put yourself in that position to make that money. So it's not that they're giving you something. You earned that position.

Dr. Boyce W.: Yeah, I earned it, but understand, for example, when I got my first job as a professor, I was the first black person they'd ever hired in the hundred year history of that department. But I was not the first smart black person to apply for that job. We've had brilliant black people since black people came into existence. But I was the first one to get that opportunity. So understand, if someone doesn't force certain people to open the door, they just won't. I'll give you a good example. When I graduated from college, I was the number one student in my whole senior class. I won awards for it and everything. Got two bachelor degrees in four years. I mean I busted my butt in school. I wanted to work on Wall Street. And it's funny because I'm staying on Wall Street this weekend and it made me think about

	this. I sent out 200 resumes to 200 Wall Street firms and got 200 rejection letters.
Angela Yee:	Wow!
Charlamagne:	Wow.
Dr. Boyce W.:	It hurt me to the core.
Charlamagne:	All you needed was one yes though.
Dr. Boyce W.:	Absolutely. One yes would have made a big difference in my life, but at the same time, sometimes not getting what you want is good. It's a lot like a relationship when you are in love with someone and she doesn't want you. Maybe a year later, you realize you're happy that she rejected you because you found somebody better.
Angela Yee:	Right?
Dr. Boyce W.:	Right. And it was the same way with that. I can't explain when you own your own stuff, when you get a chance to feel that power of being a boss, it goes far deeper than the money. If you're doing it just for the money I think you're missing like 90 percent of the equation. I mean I love money, I studied capitalism and finance. I know all about that but it's just that I breathe easier every day. I get up, I just don't crawl out of bed, and I bounce out of bed. And so I think that everybody should get a chance to feel this

	and I think we definitely have to start with our kids.
Angela Yee:	Right.
Dr. Boyce W.:	And there's no excuse to say. "Well I don't understand entrepreneurialism I can't teach this to my kids." The best university in the history of the world is called Google.com and YouTube.com. You can literally go to YouTube University and learn everything you want to know. We actually have a website called Financial Juneteenth as well that people can go to but that's one of a billion that's out -
Angela Yee:	I would recommend that over just going to random YouTube videos. Cause there's poison out there too.
Dr. Boyce W.:	Okay, there you go. Okay, I got an endorsement from Charlamagne. Thank you brother. But in all seriousness, the information is out there and sometimes really it's something small. If might be something like just saying to your kids, "Yeah one day make sure you own your own business." If you say that a few times a year, your child will hold on to that. I knew a guy who's a 27 year old millionaire and that's what he said. He said, "My dad did not ... he didn't have his own business but he just always said to me, you should have your own business." He didn't explain how to do

it. He just said this is what you should do, so that's what I did. And now he's doing really well. My dad was a cop, like your dad, and so we understood the value of hard work. I don't know about your dad but my dad was a very tough guy. He was a Vietnam Vet. I think the reason I don't have a big problem with what Damon Dash said is because my dad has a little bit of that in him.

My dad would straight up punk me when I got to feeling sorry for myself, or like, "Oh the world won't do this for me or do that for me." If you sort of shift through that energy that you're receiving that might bother you or assault your masculinity, you realize, okay maybe he has a point. Because at the end of the day, nobody really cares that much about you in this world.

Charlamagne: He's absolutely right about empowerment. He's absolutely right about ownership.

DJ Envy: But you know something, it was my dad that actually made me become an entrepreneur because like you said, my dad was a police officer so he was very hard on me. And him being so hard on me, I didn't want to work for anybody. I would never want to have a boss like that. I swear to God. So I started doing mixed tapes and started on my own and selling them because I didn't want a boss. For me, like I told Dame, radio is my passion. I love it. You know how people get up and you say you get that bounce in the morning? I'm not tired. I enjoy coming to work. There's not a day that I'm like, "Damn I got to come to work."

When I miss work too many days, I start feigning it. Like, "I have to get to work" I start calling Charlamagne, like, "Whatchu doin?" I call someone else like, "Whatchu doin? Where you at?" You know? I love this job, but there are a lot of people who don't need to be entrepreneurs. That don't have that in their heart. So that people who need to invest, what can they invest in? Because that's something that people just don't know. They don't, they scared of the stock market so they don't know what they can invest in. They hear about the stock market going up and down. They feel like real estate is too much money to put ten percent down or five percent down on a home. So what would you advise for that person that doesn't want to be an entrepreneur or that doesn't have the time, or has kids, that just wants to invest their money? What would you tell them to put their money in something that can make money? Not just a bank where they're going to make two percent out of 100 years. Something that they can possibly make some money?

Dr. Boyce W.: Well when I first got started investing, I put my money in mutual funds. It's not complex. You just go to your bank and say, "Can you

	show me some mutual funds I can invest in?" They'll show you what to do. They even have scenarios where you could set up a drip, where you take a little bit of your paycheck, it could be ten dollars, fifty dollars, whatever, and it goes in this account over time. And I can tell you this,
Angela Yee:	What about retirement?
Dr. Boyce W.:	A tax deferred plan could be the start of thinking about investing. That's what I did. I had money going into my retirement account. And believe it or not I actually, when I did finally leave my job and start my own business, my retirement account which had built up over the years, it kind of play the role of a small bank for me. There are sometimes you can't get the capital you want. Sometimes the bank won't lend it to you and you just don't have it. So sometimes I borrow against myself and whatever. What I found too though was that there were so many opportunities when it comes to investing in the black community. So many opportunities are just overlooked. And literally I was able to double and triple my money pretty quickly.
Charlamagne:	Just off the bank stuff?
Dr. Boyce W.:	Yeah -
Charlamagne:	Diversifying your portfolio.

Dr. Boyce W.: Yeah, now the mutual fund part, that is diversification. A mutual fund is not something where you're picking the stock or trying to pick the right stock at the right time. Your money is invested in thousands of stocks and really I just put my money in and I just made sure I had certain balances as far as risk. Not too much risk, not too little, and then I just left it alone.

DJ Envy: But that's longevity. Most, especially African Americans, they want their money now. Like they don't want to wait 20 years down the line to see that money come in, they want to flip their money now.

Charlamagne: Better go sell that crack! No please.

Dr. Boyce W.: Don't sell crack.

DJ Envy: Something with more risk. Like what do you advise. Because I had my money in mutual funds and bonds but you look at that money and be like, "My kid can see that." You know what I mean? But what can they invest in now that says, "You know what, try this or look at this, or maybe this might be for you." Where I could make a quicker flip.

Dr. Boyce W.: Well two things. One, there are billionaires being created every day on the internet. I mean I'm telling you, these Silicon Valley cats, they got it figured out, they create value very quickly with very little capital

	investments sometimes.
Charlamagne:	Those apps. All that social media apps, what Snap Chat, Twitter.
DJ Envy:	Those apps are killin it.
Dr. Boyce W.:	Yup, and then on top of that, I would say partner with someone that identifies a need and help fill it. It might be something as simple as, "My friend bakes cookies really good and when she goes to work and brings her cookies everybody loves them."
Charlamagne:	What's with you bald headed guys and cookies?
Dr. Boyce W.:	Ain't nothing wrong with cookies man.
Charlamagne:	Damon Dash started selling cookies too.
Dr. Boyce W.:	Oh really? Oh does he?
Charlamagne:	Yeah.
Dr. Boyce W.:	I mean maybe there's plenty of cookies, I don't know! I don't know, I like cookies. I like cookies.
Charlamagne:	The other day Dame came in saying, "My son sells cookies!"
Dr. Boyce W.:	So a lot of times ... I can tell you I made most of my money like that. Just identifying a little need and if I have a friend that wants

	to do something and they need 500 dollars to get started, I invest, I own half of the company or whatever, and then you make money that way. Most of my money has been built from small businesses that I created online and offline as opposed to the long term stuff with the stock market. So I think people should do both, a little bit of both.
DJ Envy:	But being real. Realistically right? So now you open up a business, who do you hire to run your business? Who do you hire as your employee?
Dr. Boyce W.:	Well I don't -
DJ Envy:	Do you hire African Americans or do you hire people that best suit the job?
Dr. Boyce W.:	I think we do both. I'm a big fan of hiring black people. Because people tend to hire people like them.
Charlamagne:	I know that's why a lot of times people think it's a race issue with the employee discrimination but actually it's just like, "No, I'm just hire people I relate to".
Dr. Boyce W.:	Right. Sometimes black people are the only ones who kind of fall for that lie that we shouldn't love people that are like us and support our own community. If you go to like Jewish communities and Arab

	communities, I mean they are hooking up their family members first and foremost.
Charlamagne:	Your absolutely right.
Dr. Boyce W.:	Now at the same time, you don't want to hire relatives who are going to screw up your company or ruin your relationship by doing a bad job, so there are some relatives I would never hire in a million years. But when I have an opportunity I look to the people around me first. I take care of people in my circle, in my family. Blood family or not, right? And then if I can't find somebody, then I might go outside of that. Sites like Odesk and Elance are where you can find contractors at a good price, stuff like that if you don't have a lot of money. But I'm a big fan of supporting your own. I mean why wouldn't we do that? That's really essential to survival.
Dr. Boyce W.:	A lot of people are scared of our own. I think a lot of African Americans are scared to hire our own and are fearful of our own. It's one of those things, it's like you're scared of yourself and I see that a lot.
Dr. Boyce W.:	I think sometimes the biggest supporters of white supremacy are black people actually. We truly believe that we are a flawed brand of society. Some of us. We really say things about ourselves that are disparaging. Many of us, because we don't always have a

	culture to connect to. Remember, a lot of black history doesn't even start for many of us before slavery. We have no clue what happened to us before we arrived on slave ships.
DJ Envy:	Right.
Dr. Boyce W.:	So for many of us, we might assimilate and latch our minds onto obtaining acceptance within let's say white institutions as a sign of progress. We'll say something like. "Okay, well so and so was the first black man to get into Harvard and I'm very proud of that." Which, fine, okay.
Charlamagne:	You shouldn't be proud of Harvard.
Dr. Boyce W.:	Right, but here's the thing though, you don't really hear white folks saying, "Well this is the first white man to get into Morehouse." They don't care! They don't consider assimilation or acceptance by us to be a step up. But we consider assimilation or acceptance from them to be a step up and I just don't think that that's a healthy way to thing.
Charlamagne:	I look at things like that and I think it's not the black person that's making progress, Harvard is making progress cause they finally accepting us.
Dr. Boyce W.:	Exactly. We are such a strong and capable

people, intellectually, physically and otherwise. Even if you look at sports there really is no sort of white version of Shaquille O'Neal, no white version of Kobe Bryant. I think that there is something about the fact that we survived hundreds of years of the most brutal torture ever dropped on any group of human beings on the planet. I think that's what makes people fear us. And so if you fear something, if you are a trainer of a big elephant and you know that elephant could crush you in second, what do you do? You have to control the elephant's mind from the very beginning and make him think that you're the boss. I think that's kind of what happens to us. I think that we're trained to hate ourselves so much we will kill each other, we will dog each other out, we won't support each other and I think that's a problem.

Charlamagne: *Empire?*

Dr. Boyce W.: Well I think that Lee Daniels is to some extent might be dissing all of us. Don't get me wrong. I'm not hating on people that enjoy the show, I'm not attacking people who work on the show, but here's the thing. Black men are the most incarcerated group of people on the planet. We even incarcerate more black men in America than South Africa did during the height of apartheid. Apartheid was considered the most racism regime in history and we incarcerate more

	black men than they did, what does that say about America? Right? So, given that that is true many of those incarcerations occur, many of those men are innocent and women as well. It occurs -
Charlamagne:	Everybody in jail is innocent.
Dr. Boyce W.:	Well not everybody
Charlamagne:	Well that's what they say, everybody's innocent -
Dr. Boyce W.:	But there are so many cases -
Charlamagne:	Everybody says they are.
Angela Yee:	Everybody in jail says they're innocent.
Dr. Boyce W.:	But whenever [inaudible 00:28:31] we write about some brother who went to prison in 1982 for something he didn't do, did 30 years and they gave him half a million dollars or something, like that's going to make it better. One brother in fact got nine million because he was sent to prison for a rape he did not commit, but he was raped many times in prison, caught HIV in the process -
Angela Yee:	I just saw that story. That was awful.
Dr. Boyce W.:	Yes! And on top of that the prosecutors a year later, a year after they incarcerated him found the guy who committed the crime,

locked him up but didn't release him. They kept him in prison for 30 years and he had a newborn daughter. This is the kind of atrocities, the kind of Holocaust really that we're dealing with. So, in light of that, that is the backdrop of all of this, we have to understand in many cases when that brother goes before that all white jury, a lot of those prosecutors get a conviction, all he has to do is paint some picture of this black man being a thug. And that's why George Zimmerman was released because they showed picture of Trevon smoking weed like, "Oh he was a thug." But we know George Zimmerman was the real thug, right?

Jordan Davis. When he got murdered for playing his music too loud, they painted him as a thug in the courtroom. There are a lot of -

Charlamagne:	That guy got sentenced to a lot of time.
Dr. Boyce W.:	He got his time. Thank God. But then you got Brian Banks, the football player who was falsely accused of rape who lost his whole career because of that accusation. His attorney told him, he said, "Brian, you are a big black man. If you go in front of that all-white jury, they are going to send you to prison. You're not going to get justice because you're a big black man." That's why he took the plea. A lot of brothers go to prison for taking the plea, we know this,

right?

So the questions that I ask myself is -

Charlamagne: But what about Empire?

Dr. Boyce W.: Right. I'm getting to Empire. The question I ask myself is, if you got this all-white jury many of whom don't even have any black friends, don't know a whole lot of black people, why is it so easy to convince that this black man is a scary thug?

Charlamagne: Perception.

Dr. Boyce W.: Right. Perception which comes from many times the media. So in my opinion, it doesn't mean that I hate Empire, I saw it, it's a good show. But I said, you know I have to be a conscientious objector to the consistent portrayal of black men as criminal, thug, gangster type people cause that's not who we are.

Charlamagne: I agree with you, but this is my thing too. Art reflects life, right? And I feel like guys like Lee Daniels, they're only showing us one POV of African Americans. They're not showing the guys like you. They're not showing, we need more stuff like Selma, showing guys like Martin Luther King Jr. We don't need any more slave movies, we can do without the thug experience, we've heard that a numerous amount of times in

	music and movies. But I don't think it's necessarily Lee Daniels' fault, he's just showing us one POV of African Americans.
Dr. Boyce W.:	In my opinion when I look at the trail of Lee's work, he's showing a very consistent POV that kind of shows this basement of black life. Just the most, the worse, most disgusting things that happen in the black community. But I looked at Precious, I mean I was depressed. When I walked into that -
Charlamagne:	African American horror movie!
Dr. Boyce W.:	Right. It was like, "What the hell is this man? Like are you serious?" Like this poor girl was getting crapped on the whole movie.
Charlamagne:	I hated it.
Dr. Boyce W.:	And here's the thing.
Charlamagne:	When I found out it was ... I thought it was real. But then when I found out it wasn't real, I was like, "Damn. You couldn't have a happy ending at least?"
Dr. Boyce W.:	Yeah, it reminds me of Quentin Tarantino and how his movies are so sick that you're just like, man, like what did you go through as a child? So I literally studied Lee's background, like I read his Wikipedia page in detail. I'm trying to just understand, but if

	you look at Lee's background, he's experienced some horrible shit. Excuse my French.
Angela Yee:	Right.
Dr. Boyce W.:	My bad. You know he's gone through some terrible things and the trauma, the abuse, being denied love from his family. He talks about his sister as an obese crack addict. I think when you go through that kind of trauma as a black person, which a lot of us do, you can somehow associate your blackness with just the very worst thing that could happen in a society. So what do you do then? Then you somehow might be convinced that maybe on the other side of town where the white folks live, that that's the paradise. That's where you want to be, that's where life gets good, and I think that that's unfortunate because I think there are a lot of healthy experiences that are occurring on the black community and I don't see those portrayed as regularly to me.
Angela Yee:	Well you got *Blackish* now.
Dr. Boyce W.:	Yes, I love *Blackish*.
DJ Envy:	But this is the problem though. You look at *Empire* right? Or *Love and Hip Hop* and you say, "You know what? This is not positive for my people. But it's going to make me a lot of money." Right? And this is the

problem. You say, "Well if I don't make it, somebody else gonna make it. So why don't I make it and make the money?"

Charlamagne: Why can't we just look at it like entertainment? Like how you said about white people, you said white people -

DJ Envy: As long as I make the money I could put the money into the positive things and maybe help. Maybe he's doing it and maybe not, but I look at some things like that where you look at your Love and Hip Hop and it's an F'ed up show and you look at Empire and its so many stereotypes. It pisses me off sometimes, like, they're fighting and "Tell the cops F ..." It's so stereotypical, you know when I walk out my house I feel like my neighbors are looking at me like, "Uh hmm." You know what I mean?

Charlamagne: Envy's right but how you said about white people. They don't look at white people getting into Morehouse as an accomplishment. Do you think they look at their own entertainment and think Quentin Tarantino is bad for white people? The stuff he make. The music -

Angela Yee: People are mad about The Sopranos and Mob Wives.

DJ Envy: Italians [crosstalk 00:33:17]

Angela Yee:	Do white people get upset like how we do? Like they're affecting our people.
Dr. Boyce W.:	Well I think whites have the luxury, this does come back to white privilege and white supremacy to some extent because they own the media outlets they get such a diverse array of portrayals. But I have a lot of friends in Hollywood and I'm sure you do to who will say, "You know I get tired of going into auditions and have them tell me to be the black woman with attitudes. Swing my ... talk loud, etc, or I get tired of being asked to be the black man who portrays a thug." I remember I was very proud of Idris Elba because he took a stand and was saying, "There are certain roles I just will no play, even for Tyler Perry." He was in a Tyler Perry movie. And so the thing about media to me, is that media is just one of the most powerful forms of propaganda known to man.
Charlamagne:	Malcolm X said it.
Dr. Boyce W.:	Right, it is -
Dr. Boyce W.:	Yes, I mean Hitler used media to justify the persecution and the abuse and the slaughter of the Jews. All you have to do is you paint them as menaces to society, as these fundamentally dysfunctional people, these, almost like roaches and maggots that you have to exterminate and then people will

	sign off on allowing you to exterminate them. Well it's hard to argue that that's not what's been consistently happening with black people. Even when we were being lynched on a regular basis, they didn't just lynch black people just for being black. They would always have an excuse, it would also be, "Well, he touched that white woman." or "He stole some cookies." Back to cookies.
Charlamagne:	Right.
Dr. Boyce W.:	I guess I'm going to eat some cookies after.
Charlamagne:	We got some cookies right here.
Dr. Boyce W.:	I know, I need some cookies. But so, at the end of the day I think that a lot of what we're seeing in the media, we have to make sure we don't fall for this idea that it's just entertainment. That's how propaganda works is you convince people it's just entertainment. Nothing is just entertainment. Most of the time there's an agenda. Even Lee and his producers said that, "Our goal is the blow the lid off homophobia in the black community." They understand that entertainment does have an impact on the way people think.
Charlamagne:	But that's actually true. When I heard him say that statement, I said, "I think Lee, you care more about homophobia than we do."

Dr. Boyce W.: Yeah.

Charlamagne: You know what I'm sayin? Like I ain't tripping off of it like that.

DJ Envy: But the problem is especially in our community, we idolize that. And like Charlamagne says all the time, you know we like to go to the schools and talk to the kids but growing up in Queens, I see my dad and I see my dad work mad overtime to make sure my Christmas was great and spend a lot of money to put me in Catholic School. But then I would see all the drug dealers driving up the block working an hour or two and they had the expensive cars, the nice jewelry, the women and I think for our community we look at that as making it. We don't look at the family as, I had my mother and father in the household. I had my father there on Christmas and my father never went to jail. We don't look at that so when you see some of these movies that, we talk about some of these movies, Menace to Society, and what's that movie that you just said the other day that you wanted -

Charlamagne: *Boy in the Hood.*

DJ Envy: *Boyz in the Hood.*

Charlamagne: *Juice.*

DJ Envy: *Juice* and Wesley Snipes movie?

Charlamagne:	*New Jack City*.
Dr. Boyce W.:	*New Jack City*!
DJ Envy:	*New Jack City*. We love, we love watching it and we enjoy watching those types of movies, but -
Charlamagne:	I never gave a damn about Tony Montana.
DJ Envy:	Besides *Coming to America*, I can't even think of a positive movie that -
Charlamagne:	Bill Cosby. *A Different World*.
DJ Envy:	But we don't have none of that now.
Charlamagne:	*Martin* was positive to me cause Martin had a job. Martin did radio.
Dr. Boyce W.:	He loved the black woman too. I mean that's important as well.
Charlamagne:	Yeah.
Dr. Boyce W.:	Absolutely.
DJ Envy:	Besides that on TV what do we have now?
Charlamagne:	I'm a be honest with you.
DJ Envy:	You look at Scandal it seems like the black woman's the side chic.
Angela Yee:	Its interesting because they just did an

article that I was talking about in Deadline. They were saying that, "Right now the pendulum might have swung a bit too far in the opposite direction," and that, "Before there were too few roles for actors of color in Hollywood." And now according to this article, "Basically 50% of the roles in a pilot have to be ethnic and the mandate goes all the way down to guest parts." And basically what they're saying now is that it's swung too far in the other direction.

Dr. Boyce W.: I think that could be progress. The reason I like *Blackish* is not because I believe that everything is cotton candy and cupcakes. It's because Blackish allows black people to be human. We're very diverse, heterogeneous people. Some of us are nerdy, some of us are scandalous, whatever and I just like to see stuff where you're being black is not the first thing that people will understand about your character. In fact when I went to South Africa this week, or a couple of weeks ago, I loved the fact that people didn't care that I was black because everybody was black. At that point people want to more about who you are as a person but sometimes in America, the first thing people notice is that I'm a black guy and it comes with all this baggage and all these expectations and stereotypes and I think that's a heavy burden for all of us to carry.

Charlamagne: I mean that's like that in the media too

because I'm the type of person, if I see a situation that happened between a police officer and a young black male, I don't think this is a white police officer and black male. The first thing I think is, "What happened?"

Dr. Boyce W.: Absolutely.

Charlamagne: I want a little scenario first.

Dr. Boyce W.: Yes.

Charlamagne: Before I just jump to the, "Oh he was white, he was black. It was racism."

Dr. Boyce W.: Absolutely. That's what we would call critical thinking, which we have to do and it's really important because we got so many cases that are being revealed now of black people being shot by the police and I think the biggest mistake we can make is assuming that every white cop just wakes up with a blood thirst and wants to kill black people.

Charlamagne: Yeah I don't want that kind of fear. I find myself paranoid and scared, like, "Whoa!"

Dr. Boyce W.: Yeah.

Angela Yee: At the same time you do know that racial profiling does -

Dr. Boyce W.: Absolutely. It's very very real and I was saying Envy could say, I assume you know

	some cops that worked with your dad on the force. I know from my experience, I saw the good and the bad. I've seen cops that just were good people that wanted to help. Now think about it, a good cop has a really tough job because you have to care about problems that are not yours.
Angela Yee:	Right.
Dr. Boyce W.:	A lot of times your helping people get a cat out of a tree or just help somebody find directions, you know just little things that a lot of us don't really want to do and then you put yourself in harm's way. But then you got those cops who will abuse their authority. There are many reasons to be afraid of cops. We live in a society where people assume that cops are innocent and that if you are the quote unquote criminal, that somehow the cops should get the benefit of the doubt about what happened. Right?
Angela Yee:	What else that makes if difficult is when you've had bad experiences with cops. That makes you not trust cops period.
Dr. Boyce W.:	Absolutely. I think good cops should be taking the lead in terms of helping weed out bad cops.
DJ Envy:	Absolutely.
Dr. Boyce W.:	Because it hurts all of them because we need

	good cops in the world and our community. I mean I don't think anybody want to live in the world without police officers.
Charlamagne:	Cause I don't see a black cop and be like, "He's good" and see a white cop and be like, "He's bad." I just see cop period and be like, "I'm staying away from all of them."
Angela Yee:	Away from that.
Charlamagne:	That blue wall of silence is real. Cops are threatened in many many ways, sometimes even threatened with death for speaking up. And I think that, it's the system that is really is the culprit there because you're just as likely to be abused by a black cop as by a white cop in many cases. So that's what we kind of have to deal with and not get so caught up in the black and white and not caught up in this idea that every cop who shots a black man somehow is a bad evil person. I don't think cops just get up wanting to kill people every day. That's just my theory.
DJ Envy:	But it's also media though because I look at my son, you know? We live in a nice area in Jersey, so what he sees is what's on TV. So when you look on channel 12 or channel 1 or the news channel, all you see is, young African American on TV doing bad. It never show positivity, never show positive, they'll

	say, "8 people shot in Newark, this is what the suspect looks like." "8 people shot in Paterson, 2 people shot in the Bronx, 2 people shot in Brooklyn." So my son starts to see African Americans as bad.
Charlamagne:	But you've got to show them different. I've never been the type to put that much cache into the media or entertainment. My mother and father kept -
DJ Envy:	But both [inaudible 00:40:44] dad, there's a lot of people out there that don't have parents raising them and they are raised from media and raised from music. It's out there like that and that makes it difficult.
Charlamagne:	That's what's dangerous.
DJ Envy:	And its very dangerous.
Dr. Boyce W.:	What we still have not quite figured out is that the mass incarceration epidemic that started in the 70's has obliterated the black family. This whole 72% of black children being born without a father in the house, that didn't really start until so many fathers were being sent to prison and marginalized. I'll give you one example. There's a guy I know in Chicago, Mario Lloyd. Sold some cocaine, never killed anybody, at least he wasn't convicted for anything like that.
Charlamagne:	He did kill somebody if he sold cocaine.

Dr. Boyce W.: There you go -

Charlamagne: Maybe there was a woman who overdosed -

Dr. Boyce W.: There you go.

Charlamagne: Or somebody could have killed somebody for that coke, we gotta stop saying that. Yes.

Dr. Boyce W.: Okay, okay, fair enough. He sold cocaine, people were hurt by this. Absolutely. But here's the interesting thing. When the Feds took him away, they gave him 15 life sentences for non-violent first-time offense. They locked up his mother, they locked up his sister and they locked up his brother. So the question is, when you [crosstalk 00:41:48] There you go. So when you lock up an entire family, what happens to those kids?

Angela Yee: Right.

Dr. Boyce W.: 20 years later Mario's son gets murdered in the same neighborhood that his father used to deal drugs in. You need those role models there. You can't think a community is going to prosper when your killing off all the men. It just doesn't happen.

Charlamagne: It's that none of this would have happened if he would have never sold coke. And I mean I used to sell dope, but it's just that simple.

Dr. Boyce W.: But, right. I agree. I agree. Breaking the law

	is wrong. We all agree on that. But the punishment has to fit the crime. I mean 15 life sentences? I don't understand that. Another brother, Joe [inaudible 00:42:22] got 40 years for possessing a gram of crack. Come on now, and if you really want to see -
Recording:	That's ridiculous.
Dr. Boyce W.:	If you really want to see people breaking the law, if you really want to see people possessing drugs, go to a college campus on the weekend. But I guarantee you they will never raid a college campus they way they'll go up in the hood and lock everybody up.
DJ Envy:	And not only that. You said that people shouldn't sell drugs and I know this is going to be a tough statement but I understand it at times. Like you said, you just named a young man that gotta take care of his grandmother, his mother and his brother. He's the man of the house -
Charlamagne:	Get a job.
DJ Envy:	And you say get a job but McDonalds making 9 dollars an hour if not going to pay -
Angela Yee:	Part of what makes that hard is the community, the environment that you grew up in. So if everybody around you is doing

	something and that's how you were raised and that's what everybody is doing, sometimes it's hard.
Charlamagne:	This is what I don't understand. I don't understand it because I've seen the outcome. The outcome is jail or death. That's it!
Dr. Boyce W.:	Right.
Charlamagne:	That's it! So that's what I don't understand. Insanity is doing the same thing over and over expecting different results.
Angela Yee:	But I know people who have said, "Listen. I grew up in this terrible neighborhood, that's what everybody's doing, that's, all my role models were doing that. Everybody around me that, it just seem normal." And so that's what I think makes it difficult sometimes for people. And then you give them 15 consecutive life sentences and he never had a chance to do something else or experience something else to get a second chance.
DJ Envy:	But there's always Jamal that didn't get the life sentences that made the money and got -
Dr. Boyce W.:	Charlamagne.
DJ Envy:	The Charlamagne that didn't -
Charlamagne:	But I don't think people getting those types of opportunities no more.

DJ Envy:	But change the law.
Dr. Boyce W.:	Here's another interesting thing, when you talk about that scenario of working at McDonalds. I live on the south side of Chicago and a lot of those kids just cannot find jobs anywhere. In fact there are some neighborhoods where a black youth or black man especially has an easier time getting a gun than he has of getting an education, or getting a decent job. So I think that is part of the issue as well and then I think a fundamental question to really ask is, we know teenagers, are just pretty stupid at times. Not dumb, but a lot of us did dumb stuff when we -
Angela Yee:	Of course. Part of growing up.
Dr. Boyce W.:	Antisocial stuff, right. And so the question to me is, what's the cost of making a mistake? Why is it that for some people in our society, like you look at somebody like a George Bush. That's what I was talking about, what if George Bush were a black man -
Dr. Boyce W.:	Thank you brother. I appreciate that. What would have happened if George Bush were a poor black kid in Cabrini Green Projects in Chicago and made the same mistakes he made?
Dr. Boyce W.:	Right. He'd be dead or he'd be in prison. She

	certainly would never have had the chance to become president and make up for his mistakes. Right?
Charlamagne:	Actually, he became president and made more mistakes, but go ahead.
Dr. Boyce W.:	Well there you go. Well he's a war criminal. We know that right? To me, I think that we have to really question why we have a society where for certain people one mistake at the age of 17 or 18 can destroy you for life.
Charlamagne:	I agree with that.
Dr. Boyce W.:	My older brother, he was really my uncle but he was like my older brother, went to prison at 17. I don't know what happened when he was in prison, but I know bad things can occur. All I know is that when he came out he just wasn't right mentally. He only did two years but prison is such a nightmare. People are being tortured in prison. Think about it.
Charlamagne:	Getting raped.
Dr. Boyce W.:	Getting raped! And we make jokes about that, that's not funny! Rape is not funny! It's not!
Charlamagne:	Man rape is a little funny sometimes.
Angela Yee:	No it's not. It's never funny. That's a

	nightmare.
Dr. Boyce W.:	It's a nightmare. It's torture. It's an abuse of human rights. And so we put people through that and we think somehow you're going to come out rehabilitated. We know that's not going to happen.
Charlamagne:	No!!
Dr. Boyce W.:	And you're marginalized for life, you can't get a job. Really, the truth here is that we live in a country now were incarceration has become profitable. So I think now we have a country where people don't really want you to get away from the system.
Charlamagne:	Stock market -
Dr. Boyce W.:	The private prisons, exactly!
Damon Dash Clip:	You need to come up here more often man.
Dr. Boyce W.:	Id' be glad to.
Charlamagne:	Let's play one more Damon Dash clip. Play the saving money clip, cause you know, cause you could really watch him as the jack of all trades but he's really good at finance.
Dr. Boyce W.:	And nine to fives aren't good because you're hustling for a weekend.
Charl. Clip:	You act like you never worked your way up to a position, you didn't just jump -

Damon Dash Clip:	No I never did. I never had a job.
Charl. Clip:	But you didn't jump out as a tycoon.
Damon Dash Clip:	Yes I did. Yes I did. I went and grabbed it. I flipped.
Charl. Clip:	From the womb?
Damon Dash Clip:	Yes, from the womb I was Damon Dash the day I was born.
Charl. Clip:	But you didn't have everything you have now from the womb.
Damon Dash Clip:	The way I got it was not by a job. I got it putting up my own money, like one day I'll have a lot of money, and then the next day I don't. You know why? Because I put it all in the street. You keep saying, "Yo, you just started, you didn't ... No dog, I always flipped. " I don't put up money. Saving money's for suckers. I have so much confidence in me, that I flip and 20 years later I'm still a boos and you still got a job.
Charlamagne:	I would love to close on that, what do you think of that?
Dr. Boyce W.:	I think that the goal of being a boss is a good objective to have. I don't think that everybody has to be Damon Dash. There are many people that are bosses who have philosophies different from Dame. I like the way he just awakens the sleeping dragon

which is bold commentary. I mean Damon Dash is Damon Dash. He's always going to be that person. But there's not Jay Z without Damon Dash, you know, that type of thing. We have to give him credit for that. His desire to take risks sometimes has led to tremendous fortune and sometimes some misfortune. But remember, you can't diss Dame's commentary per se just because he's not always doing as well as he might have hoped. Remember Donald Trump claimed bankruptcy four times.

Charlamagne: Right. So saving money's for suckers?

Dr. Boyce W.: Now the idea of saving money being for suckers, no, I mean come on, you can't say that. But I would say that simply saving money doesn't make send. I think saving -

Angela Yee: And have it just sit there.

Dr. Boyce W.: Right, saving and investing is really the best approach. The idea at the end of the day is find ways to keep your money in your pocket and put it into things that are going to empower you. Eventually your money has to start working for you and everybody can do it. Get out of the what I call slave mentality. The slave mentality to me is when you would go work 10-12 hours a day because somebody told you to come to work and they're going to give you a minimum wage paycheck. But when it comes to working half of that time to achieve goals for yourself, where it be educationally or entrepreneurial or whatever. You can't put in the time. You ain't got time. You want to go get turnt up, you want to watch Basketball Wives or whatever and that doesn't make sense to me. Why would you spend more time building somebody else's dream and no time building your own. That makes no sense to me.

Charlamagne: I always tell interns, interns be like, "Well how do I have time to go to school, and have a job, and do an internship?" It's a 168 hours in a week. You invest time in what you want to invest time in.

Dr. Boyce W.: That's right.

Charlamagne: Period.

Dr. Boyce W.: There you go.

DJ Envy: Well there you have it. Dr. Boyce Watkins. We appreciate you joining us.

Charlamagne: Yeah you gotta come more often man.

Dr. Boyce W.: Thank you brother. I appreciate the invitation.

Charlamagne: Anytime you're in NY. Cause financial literacy is something that I think more of us need. Especially after what I've heard in the past couple of weeks. Financial tips from

	people, I'm like I have no clue what you're talking about .
Dr. Boyce W.:	Well I respect you guys. And Charlamagne I've always respected you. Back when we was doing the Wendy Show man you ... Charlamagne always respected me even when nobody else did. That's why I love this brother. Thank you.
Charlamagne:	Thank you brother.
DJ Envy:	All right. It's The Breakfast Club Dr. Boyce Watkins

CHAPTER 10

CREATING MULTIGENERATIONAL WEALTH

There is a proverbial saying that "Children are the future." This statement is only partially true. If we see our children as the future then what is their purpose right now? Because we have not always seen children as viable parts of our community—children should be seen and not heard—we sometimes silence them and do not include them when we are making plans for the future, especially as it relates to money.

I mentioned earlier that our children are watching us. Knowing this, what are we going to do about it? First and foremost, we need to acknowledge that most black people know very little about generational wealth. Maybe a few of us were the beneficiaries of life insurance policies, Big Momma's house or PaPa's car.

Although these items are valuable, it's not the same as being on the receiving end of an estate, a trust, or a business entity. If properly planned and structured, one trust could support several generations of an entire family. It is how major tycoons ensure that their heirs will have access to the resources and the lifestyles that they desire.

Now, I know that systemic racism prevented us from having the same access and opportunities—it is one of the reasons I am a strong proponent of reparations—but I want us to think about what we are doing right now to prepare for future generations.

Think about your own child or grandchild. What are you leaving them?

When we don't prepare and we don't pass down our wealth to the next generation then that generation and the ones after it often have to start from scratch. It becomes one big cycle.

The key to breaking the cycle is understanding how to generate, manage, and preserve wealth. Recently, I was talking to somebody and I said that I think every child, every black child in America should know how to start a business by the time they're 12 or 13 years old.

Well, you know the first person came along and said something like there's nothing wrong with working under somebody. I also hear other people will say that, but I'm shaming people who work for other people. I'm not shaming anything. I think someone else said that there's nothing wrong with working for somebody else; all that matters is that you give good customer service et cetera.

Now, let me clarify. I don't think there's anything wrong with working under somebody else if you're happy doing that. There's nothing wrong with that. However, there is something wrong with not having a plan B.

The fact is that you can't go through life as a black person with all of the vulnerabilities that you have as a person of color, all of the risks, all of the threats to your happiness, to your well-being, to your freedom, to your life, and to your safety without some financial protection, without some backup, or without some insurance.

I see business ownership as a form of insurance that black people should have. Every black person should tell their child, get your insurance by making sure you know how to start a business just in case that white man isn't hiring no more. Have a plan B because I meet too many highly educated and ambitious black people who tell me that they can't get a job in their fields. When I hear this, I say "Well that's your damn problem right there."

Yes, it sounds mean, but it is not. This is what I call tough love and sometimes, the truth does not make us feel better.

Here's why I am mot very sympathetic when I hear this. Jobs are created. Jobs are built. Jobs are created by somebody else. Jobs don't just fall out of the sky. They're not delivered by a stork.

The real question is who's doing the creating? White folks have often created the jobs that they give to you. Who says you can't create your own job?

Imagine if you're eating food every day and you still say, "I'm hungry." The only way you can eat is if somebody over there creates the food and feeds it to me. That means they grew it; they cooked it; they skinned it; and they're feeding it to me. However, they won't feed me if I don't pay them for it. The thing is that when somebody else is creating your job for you, you're going to pay for that position in some capacity

In fact, you're going to literally pay with your freedom, with your happiness, with your well-being, and in many instances, with your freedom of speech. Black folks, when you buy your jobs from white people, you end up paying with your soul. You end up feeling indebted to white people. You end up feeling unhappy, and you end up feeling stressed out.

What I don't understand is why you would want to pass that disease down to your children. Why you would want to pass that mental illness down to the people you love?

I'm not dissing anyone who works for other people. We all work for someone, I mean not all of us, I know I worked for people before and I'm not saying it's a bad thing. Even to this day, there are times when I go give a speech and I think of myself as a person who's working for the person who's paying me to do that speech. I am very clear about that.

I feel like I'm working for them at that moment, and I'm okay with that. I don't feel bad, but you know what the difference is, I know I have options. I know that I'm only going to let you go so far with me before I say, "You know what, that's all right, I'm going to get on out of here, I got somewhere else I could be right now and I am going to get there."

Imagine if I had nowhere else to be or nowhere else to go. Imagine if I needed them and they started disrespecting me. Unless I have a Plan B, I have no options. I'm stuck, and when you feel trapped and stuck, you feel depressed. It is also when you start to feel stressed. We have many people in our communities whose behaviors are directly correlated to their working in jobs that they loathe.

That is when people seek destructive outlets like drugs and alcohol, clubbing on the weekends, sex with everything that moves, and other forms of escapism. Black people are always in the midst of escapism. That's why we love comedy so much, in my opinion. We look for anything that will help us escape the trap that we were trained to walk right into and stay in, even though there is a way out—much like the rat study I discussed earlier in the book.

I'm going to just be honest with you, most people are not going to get it. Most people don't understand it.

Why is this you might ask?

Some people start playing a line dance; everybody wants to line dance. Everybody wants to party and everybody wants to laugh, but then when the crisis hits, I become one of the first people that they come to saying "What are you going to do to help, Dr. Boyce. We don't know what to do; this is horrible."

I understand why it's horrible, but an ounce of prevention is worth a pound of cure. A lot of times, unfortunately, we are trained to be reactive instead of proactive. You're more likely to react to the tragedy that you just experienced than you are to be proactive and respond to the pending tragedy that will occur if you don't prepare and get ahead of it, even though this will require more work and energy in the long haul.

The same is true as it relates to generational wealthy. Sitting at daddy's funeral crying or complaining at the gravesite is too late, especially when there are ways that we can end the cycle of financial unpreparedness.

My argument is that when you talk about children, you have to be proactive not reactive. Every child before the age of 12 should know how to start a business. We have courses in the Black Business School for children (blackmillionairesoftomorrow.com.) We also have the Black Financial Leadership Program (blackfinancialleadership.com). We also have another program for black financial superstars which has a lower monthly fee. All of these, student-friendly, courses are in the Black Business School (theblackbusinessschool.com). Whether it is our program or someone else's, make sure your child is getting the basics because it's a war out here. It's not easy out here.

I am such a proponent of preparing young people because I have heard the horror stories of families that have been destroyed because of money. The reason black people get beat down so badly, spiritually and psychologically, is because we don' have access to the money that we need to get ahead. In other words, we don't have capital. We don't understand capital well enough to know where it is and know how to go get it.

That was just on my mind when I heard a brother say that there was nothing wrong with working with somebody else. I don't think there is anything wrong with working for other people, I'm just saying that there is something wrong with not having a backup plan. Any idiot, any fool knows options have value.

The first thing we learn in finance is option pricing theory. It means that options always have a nonnegative value, meaning that you never go wrong. You'll never go wrong when you have more options. So create options for yourself. When I created options, I became a much happier, much freer black man.

If you're younger than me, and I hope that a lot of you are, focus on the options. If you are older than me, focus on options. It is never too late to get ahead.

Always focus on something else you could be doing in case the first thing does not work out for you. Whenever you have options, you will do better. Think about a time when you were hungry. What determined what you ate? Was it the amount of money you had to spend or something that you had a taste for?

More than likely, when money is not an option, you are in a position to buy what you want and not what you have to. Wouldn't you like for your heirs to live where they want and not where they have to?

Also when you have options, you're not so mad about an option that somebody 'took away' from you. In other words, when it comes to life, one's finances, and one's legacy, have options. Don't sit around worrying about something you can't or don't have access to. Options matter.

And you don't have to be a rocket scientist to figure out what your options are. There are a wealth of resources available to you—many of which have been referenced in this book.

We recently filmed *The Secrets of Black Financial Intelligence* (check out the trailer at blackfinancialintelligence.com). In this documentary, we look at strategies and principles that will help you get ahead. We pull back the mask so that you can see how financial literacy can become a normal part of your existence and your children's.

As you know, I always love teaching; this is a dream come true—working with and transforming the lives of black people every day—and this film is no different.

If we start early on helping our children understand commerce, investing, and the stock market, they will never find themselves working for someone else unless they want to. Unfortunately, I know too many miserable people who hate their jobs.

I just feel sorry for my friends in academia who were never introduced to the fact that they could create their own careers outside of the university. However, we can raise up a new generation that is better prepared to decide what is going to work best for them as opposed to being told what they have to do.

A lot of black people, unfortunately, are trapped like little slaves because they do not have a plan B and they rely so heavily upon their jobs to sustain them that they can't see life beyond next week's pay check, no matter the size.

They're tricked into committing their lives to a system that doesn't work in their favor and when the system doesn't pay out for them, they end up stuck, or worse, hopeless. They end up with a singular use of their ability, which is, ultimately, to make other people rich.

Conversely, when you learn to understand entrepreneurship and understand markets, you learn how to create opportunities. The key is to drill and to drill down on a consistent basis. Let's use the financial literacy flash cards as an example.

I would challenge you to have the entire family go over the terms. Make it a game where the person who gets the most correct actually wins something. Perhaps he/she can determine which stock the family should invest in. As children go through each tern, they will eventually commit them to their working memory. This is how knowledge is created and can be recalled and applied in future situations.

You can also use the terms and show them real-world examples or watch a news program to talk about how the stock market impacts other parts of our lives. The best part is that you can quiz them in a way that is both academically driven and fun.

The added bonus is that this creates additional opportunities to bond and you are passing down another form of wealth and that's intellectual wealth. Your child's ability to use both his/her newfound financial wisdom and intellectual wisdom will give him/her a definite, and tangible, advantage. Who doesn't want our children to be ahead for once?

Well, I know who doesn't, but they are probably not reading this book either.

I like introducing new information in practical ways because I really think with kids, we've got to make it natural. In so many words, go ahead and brainwash those little suckers—don't make it tedious. You may think brainwash is too strong of a term here. But, I challenge you to listen to 30 minutes' worth of the most popular songs out right now and you will understand why 'brainwashing' is not strong enough of a word.

The reality is that the rest of the world is already trying to brainwash your kids. And what they are trying to tell them is not good. They want your children to see themselves as being inferior and to think that entertaining other people is their only pathway to success.

I'm telling you now grab a hold of their brains before everybody else does. I'm a big fan of brain washing your kids as long as you also give them critical thinking and some free will.

You're not forcing them to be something they don't want to do, but drill ideas in their head that will give them freedom. You can't give anybody anything more valuable than freedom.

It makes me really think a little bit about basketball. When I learned how to dribble with my left hand and I learned how to do spin moves, I felt free.

I felt like I could do whatever I wanted with the ball as opposed to when I could only dribble with my right hand and I could only go one way. At first, I only had a couple of moves, but when I learned how to be flexible with my skillset, I felt like the court was my domain. I could do whatever I wanted. My new skill set gave me more options. Life is the same way.

When you pick up multiple skills, you have a Swiss army knife of options that lie in front of you that allows you to do whatever you want, so get the skills. The answers are out there.

Don't spend too much time feeling sorry for yourself. That's not going to do you any good. I hate to break the news to you, but don't nobody feel sorry for you and no one will feel sorry for your children if they continue in the same direction.

Let me share the story of a young man who embodies what can happen if we connect with our children and teach them about being owners early in life.

Jaylen Bledsoe is a young man who literally used his skills to secure his financial future and he did it without a ball in his hand or a mic. In other words, he secured his future on his own terms.

While just 15-yeasrs old and a sophomore in high school, he started his own tech company. He has discovered entrepreneurship as his calling. As a result, he is his own man, and a millionaire because of it.

Jaylen says that he started his firm when he was 12-years old. Jaylen's company, Bledsoe Technologies, is now worth an estimated $3.5 million. This means that if he manages his wealth in the right way, he will be set for life.

Jaylen doesn't spend his time memorizing lyrics from rappers, smoking weed or chasing girls on Saturday nights. Yes, these are stereotypes, but this is the lifestyle that some of our young men are drawn to.

Instead, he spends his time chasing paper, pursuing his dreams and positioning himself for a truly empowered existence. Personally, I'm proud of him. I can also see that he is the beneficiary of good parents and role models. Our kids are like products off an assembly line. The outcomes we see in kids Jaylen's age are direct products of what they've been exposed to on a daily basis. It's just as easy to manufacture a businessman as it is to manufacture a thug.

Jaylen's company does web design and other forms of IT consulting for companies located mainly in the Midwest. He actually reminds me of another young person I once met named Emerson Spartz, the founder of Spartz Media. Spartz is not African American, but both of these young men serve as powerful templates for what our boys can become if given the right guidance.

When I spoke with Emerson, we both agreed that around the age of 12, we probably had ADHD. But we also both agreed that, while ADHD gets you in trouble in school, it can actually be beneficial to have a mind that races from one good idea to the next. Personally, my short attention span caused me to struggle in school until I gained my footing in college.

High school felt like prison to me, and my horrible grades reflected that sentiment. But, going back to generational wealth, my family and other adults, passed down a wealth of information to me and my siblings.

Emerson's parents, in particular, decided to take him out of the school system altogether. But not only were they going to home school their son, they also decided that they weren't going to force him to learn any particular subject the way a traditional school would have required of him.

Instead, Emerson's parents focused on making sure that their child could read well, communicate in writing, and do math, which is pretty much what any person needs to know in order to succeed in life. I've rarely seen anyone struggle in their profession because they've never read old English literature or learned the Periodic Table in Chemistry.

So, basically, Emerson's parents allowed him to study whatever he wanted, which sounds almost insane. They also required him to read a biography of a successful person every day to get a vision for his future. Before long, Emerson, like a lot of kids, gained a strong interest in Harry Potter.

He then went on to found Mugglenet.com, the largest Harry Potter site in the world. So, just like Jaylen, Emerson was a 15-year old millionaire. He is now a 26-year old genius with a natural and burning desire to learn new things. He's been featured in *Inc Magazine* and was a New York Times best-selling author by the age of 19. Speaking to him was like talking to other college professors in academia.

I know our young people can accomplish the same.

Young men like Jaylen and Emerson define the vision of what we're seeking to do with the group of educators we've gathered around the country for our homeschooling initiative at Your Black World. The public school system is failing our children miserably, especially black boys, turning potential leaders into tiny men with low self-esteem.

This has produced a state of emergency where, for every Jaylen

Bledsoe, we produce a thousand wannabe rappers, basketball players, and prison inmates. I must be entirely honest when I say that our future leadership will come from those young people who are accustomed to being creative, innovative, and original. They will also be young people who fully grasp the importance of money.

Public school systems have become a virus, infecting millions of our boys with the disease of complacent mediocrity. With each additional day of education, they become more deeply socialized into the mental health crisis that undermines their ability to become strong husbands and fathers. They then enter into an economic system that is not wired to give them employment, even when they've made good choices and obtained several years of post-secondary education; as a result, black men have the highest rates of unemployment, incarceration and homicide in the entire country. Let's face it: This nation is not designed for most black men to be successful and a thousand marches on Washington will never change that.

My suggestion on this issue is simple: 1) Every black child in America should be home schooled, even if they go to school someplace else, and 2) Every black child in America should be taught the basics of how to run their own business.

This is the cornerstone for creating generational wealth.

Homeschooling may not mean taking your child out of school every day, but it does mean using the time that your child is not in school to teach him skills he will need to be a successful adult: The basics of black history, how to be a good parent, how to buy a home, etc. Teaching your child about financial literacy is a form of home schooling.

In other words, it means being a truly educated human being with adequate life skills and the ability to engage in critical thinking. Critical thinking can make the difference between life and death, poverty, and prosperity: Nearly every black man runs into a George Zimmerman at some point in his life, whether it's a white racist trying to harm him or another black man trying to put him in the grave. Critical thinking protects us from dangers we deal with every single day.

Secondly, being an entrepreneur doesn't mean not working for anyone else, but it does mean having alternative streams of revenue so that you are not enslaved by a corporation that causes you to check your freedom and self-esteem at the door.

That way, when situations call for you to stand up, you're not faced with a corporate overseer telling you to sit right back down. Living paycheck-to-paycheck, deep in debt, on one stream of income is a surefire pathway to a lifetime of socioeconomic servitude.

A few years ago when I spoke at Medgar Evers College in New York with Dr. Cornel West, Dr. Wilmer Leon (Howard University) and others, our goal was to introduce a new paradigm of thought as it pertains to how we go about developing our youth. They must be prepared to survive and compete in a world that doesn't always love them, and have the skills necessary to overcome obstacles that they will most likely face in their path.

We MUST create more Jaylen Bledsoes and fewer Lil Waynes. The truth is that both of these young men are geniuses, and both of them know how to work hard. The difference is that one of these men is a net asset to his community and the other is a blatant liability. One of these men is positioned for freedom and the other has been pre-assigned to psychological slavery.

One of them is going to live long and prosper, while the other one might be dead before the age of 35. Both of these men are prototypes, and every prototype can be replicated with the thoughtful design of pre-determined structural and environmental factors. Don't believe me?

Check out Rosz Akins and the Carter G. Woodson Academy in Kentucky, where she manufacturers extraordinary young black men who are equipped to become world leaders in politics, business, science and everything else. This DOES NOT happen by accident.

None of our destinies happen by accident; we make choices that influence what we are able to do now and in the future. Part of the reason I do what I do right now and part of the reason you all might hear me say or write in ways that others deem controversial is because I feel it from the bottom of my heart.

I remember that pain, I know what it's like when you're going through it and you feel like nobody is really there to help you out, but we can lessen the black wealth gap between black and white people. One of the most powerful ways that we do that is through our children.

America incarcerates more black men on a per capita basis than South Africa did during the height of apartheid. In this country, a prison cell and a casket are being built for every black boy on the day he is born. If we do not change the trajectory of that child's life at an early age, then their fate is already sealed.

Not only do our boys and girls have the tools to survive all enemies foreign and domestic, they have the power to thrive and conquer when their energies are channeled in the right direction. Our community MUST regain control of this process, and we must not take "no" for an answer.

Our children can be intellectual trendsetters, financial gurus, tech leaders, and business owners, we just have to provide them with the resources. What we don't want to do is have them inherit our debt, our bad spending habits, and our willingness to plan for the future.

Of course this does not apply to everyone, but it applies to enough of us that it is worth mentioning that not everything that we inherit is positive or affirms us as human beings.

And this brings me to one of the most practical ways that you can set your children up so that they don't have to start from scratch. It boggles my mind that we are willing to spend $30 dollars a month on leisure activities, but we won't buy life insurance that will assist our children with our end-of life expense, our funerals, and our debt.

Even more importantly, we can make sure that our children can celebrate our legacies and not be burdened by our poor choices or our lack of poor planning.

In this day and age with access to technology and the internet, there is no excuse for not doing your research and determining what policy and what amount is going to be most beneficial for you and your children. Fortunately, it is not any more complicated than that. Yes, it may require some short term sacrifices, but think of something that you spend a dollar a day on? If you saved that money, what could you do with it? How could you use it to help your heirs?

There are numerous black owned insurance agencies that will provide you with your needs, so there really is no excuse. Black Insurance agents like Yolanda Spivey, owner of Michael Whitney

& Associates (www.mwhitney.com), are willing to work with you because they understand the importance of having life insurance as it relates to generational wealth. Just recently Ms. Spivey wrote an article where she talked about Master P, the music mogul.

Master P is an example of what can happen when we leave our children with the resources that they need to create or launch their own businesses. Much of his financial success is because Master P's grandfather left him with a $10,000 insurance policy. The New Orleans rapper then used that insurance policy to start *No Limit Records*. He hired many of his family members and others from impoverished sections of the city. Over the years, he created a music, movie, and fashion empire. That $10,000 financial seed all manifested into millions of dollar in liquid assets.

Think about it. If Master P had not acquired that money from his grandfather then there is a strong possibility that he, his children, and his future grandchildren would not access to generational wealth. One simple, and some might even say small, life insurance policy was the catalyst for this.

My point is you don't have to be a millionaire or a multi-millionaire to set your children up to become millionaires of the future. Whether it's through investing in a class, starting a business that you plan to leave to them, getting a life insurance policy, or establishing a trust fund, the most important component of generational wealth is that we have to be intentional and we have to be deliberate.

We can position our children to become financially secure

If you are able bodied and intelligent and you make money and you don't buy life insurance then shame on you. I'm going to make fun of you. I'm going to make fun of you after you're dead; I'm not kidding. Because it doesn't make any sense. Why would you leave your children destitute? Why would you do that? Why would anybody do that to their family?

Your children should not be in the church begging everybody from the front of the church to take up a collection so they can bury you. No. Buy you some life insurance because it doesn't cost that much. There are other forms of insurance as well, obviously health insurance. A lot of people won't quit their job and start a business because they're scared of the insurance issue. With e-commerce, you have options.

Well there are tons of companies that have insurance products built specifically for entrepreneurs. It's not that hard to get insurance, so don't let insurance be the reason that you don't quit your job. I just don't think that's a good reason for most people. For most reasonably healthy people, there's no excuse.

As we think about what it means to create and pass on black American money, I want to leave you with a final thought. Our success as a people today and in the future is born out of what we do right now. There is great urgency and significance in the choices that we make because they don't just affect us; they impact our future as a people.

As you think about some of the key points that I have addressed in this book, I hope that you are encouraged and that you are inspired to have a healthier relationship with your finances. For us to build the nation and community we desire, we must all find our own version of fearlessness. We must stop believing that receiving love from condescending white liberals is the only thing protecting us from slavery. We must stop believing that working for our oppressors will give us our only pathway to survival. We must stop playing checkers and learn that the world is run by those who master the game of chess.

Black people are the strongest and most capable people on this planet, but unfortunately, our greatness is often pushed into the shadows of unimaginable terror, trauma, and apprehension that leaves us spiritually paralyzed. It's hard to climb mountains when you have no legs, and many of us receive amputations at birth.

But we can be stronger as we enter a new chapter in America. It is only by coming together and confronting the chains that bind us that black people can be strong and united in this generation and the next.

Black American Money 2

ABOUT THE AUTHOR

Dr. Boyce D. Watkins is one of the leading financial scholars and social commentators in America. He advocates for education, economic empowerment and social justice and has changed the definition of what it means to be a Black scholar and leader in America.

He is one of the founding fathers of the field of Financial Activism – The objective of creating social change through the use of conscientious capitalism. He is a Blue Ribbon Speaker with Great Black Speakers, Inc. and one of the most highly sought after public figures in the country.

In addition to publishing a multitude of scholarly articles on finance, education and black social commentary, Dr. Watkins has presented his message to millions, making regular appearances in various national media outlets, including CNN, Good Morning America, MSNBC, FOX News, BET, NPR, Essence Magazine, USA Today, The Today Show, ESPN, The Tom Joyner Morning Show and CBS Sports.

Educationally, Dr. Watkins earned BA and BS degrees with a triple major in Finance, Economics and Business Management. In college, he was selected by the Wall Street Journal as the Outstanding Graduating Senior in Finance. He then earned a Masters Degree in Mathematical Statistics from University of Kentucky and a Ph.D. in Finance from Ohio State University and was the only African-American in the world to earn a PH.D. in Finance during the year 2002. He is the founder of The Black Wealth Bootcamp, The Black Business School and The Your Black World coalition, which have a collective total of 300,000 subscribers and 1.4 million social media followers world-wide.

Made in the USA
Lexington, KY
21 March 2017